Ernest Mandel

EUROPE VS. AMERICA

Contradictions
of Imperialism

New York and London

Introduction 5

1. Europe and America 7
2. International Concentration of Capital 18
3. The Relative Superiority of American Firms 30
4. Interpenetration of Capital in the EEC 44
5. The Nation State Today 56
6. Britain's Entry into the Common Market 68
7. The Division of the World Market 80
8. The International Monetary Crisis 93
9. The Future of Supranational Institutions 108
10. The Working Class and Inter-Imperialist Competition 122
11. The Socialist Alternative 134

Bibliography 155

Introduction

Never in human history has a country exercised global power comparable to the United States at the end of the Second World War. No power ever lost absolute supremacy so quickly. The 'American Century' did not last ten years.

Since the collapse of the Chiang Kai-shek regime on the mainland of China, ever since the Russians ended the American nuclear monopoly, the Americans have never stopped asking themselves how this happened. The causes of the relative decline of US hegemony remain a mystery to most American specialists and politicians because they refuse to judge history from the viewpoint which sees the origins, rise and fall of states and societies as ultimately determined by objective laws. They prefer to explain away the conundrums with plots – 'communist agents' who gave away the secrets of nuclear weapons and power in China to 'the Reds' – or they speak of the loss of the pioneer spirit which must now be reawakened by some new 'frontier'. But neither exorcism nor *a priori* reflections on comparative national psychology can unravel the tangled skein formed by the technological, economic, and military upheavals and social revolutions which have taken place in the last twenty years on a global scale. Only the unravelling of each of these phenomena can produce an explanation of the erosion of America's world supremacy.

The original manuscript of this study was finished at the end of December 1967 and the German edition was published in March 1968. Two months later a revolutionary upheaval broke out in France, confirming the inevitability of a revolt against the authoritarian structure of big business, the economy, and bourgeois society as a whole, as forecast in the last chapter. There seemed no reason to modify this book in the light of what had happened in France, but a few notes have been added to emphasize those aspects of the events which tally with our analysis. A series of facts which arose in the first half of 1969, concerned with the international concentration of capital, its resultant problems and its internal contradictions, have been treated similarly.

Empirical data on the subject multiply so quickly that this study could ideally be revised two or three times a year. It need only be said that the devaluation of the franc in August 1969 vindicates the analysis of Gaullism advanced here; while the revaluation of the D-mark a few months later, in effect equivalent to a concealed devaluation of the dollar, was a further striking expression of the altered relationship between the most powerful European capitalist economy and the United States. The most recent events have thus only confirmed the theses of this book.

January 1970   E.M.

Chapter 1
Europe and America

Though we must beware of over-simplification, if we seek a common denominator for the erosion of American power, we can say that, after having benefited from the law of unequal development for a century, the United States is now becoming its victim.

American capitalism, unencumbered by feudal or semi-feudal vestiges, and forced by relative labour shortage and a huge reserve of 'free land' to employ the most sophisticated technology,[1] was able in a relatively short period – which only began at the end of the Civil War towards 1870 – to

1. Because for a long time American workers had the possibility of becoming independent farmers on land which belonged to no one, thus escaping proletarianization, their wages have always been well above those of their European counterparts. American industry, if it wished to be internationally competitive, could only accept these higher wages by increasing the productivity of labour through superior technology (in Marxist terminology: the production of relative surplus value). The continual departure of the best paid workers to the frontier to become farmers or artisans gave the American proletariat a discontinuous character which in its turn slowed down the creation of class consciousness. In addition, it lacked its own revolutionary traditions because the 'United States had no history'; in other words, there had never been any need for a major bourgeois revolution to rid society and the economy of the vestiges of feudalism. There is an early attempt to interpret the meaning of certain characteristics of the American proletariat in

close up the industrial gap between itself and Britain. America's greater productivity, assisted in particular by her supplies of raw materials which were generally superior to those of her rivals, gave her the whip hand in international competition between herself and the imperialist powers of Great Britain, Germany, Japan, France and Italy (Austro-Hungary and Russia being, before the First World War, of minor importance). [2]

Developments in world iron production are a good illustration of this change. In 1880 Great Britain still produced half the world's crude steel output and contributed 80% of the world iron exports. In 1893 she was overtaken by Germany who produced twice as much between 1908 and 1913. Despite this, by the beginning of the last decade of the nineteenth century America had moved up amongst the leaders and by 1900 was the leading exporter on the world mar-

---

Engels's letter to Mrs Wischnewetsky on 3 June 1886 (Marx / Engels, *Selected Correspondence*, Martin Lawrence, London, 1934, pp. 448–9) and in a letter to Sorge, 6 January 1892. Marx had already commented on the origins of high American wages in *Wages, Price and Profit*. There is a useful reference list of liberal writers on this subject in W. E. Rappard's book, *The Secret of American Prosperity*, Greenberg, New York, 1955 (translated from the French). It was Hegel, in his *Introduction to the Philosophy of History*, who was the first to draw attention to the role of the 'frontier' in American history or, more specifically, to 'the absence of history' in the United States. Trotsky advanced a further consideration in *Europe and America* (published by the Fourth International in 1943), pointing out that the European colonists in America were in general the most industrious, resilient and active elements of the European population – those who tried to escape repression during the revolutions of the sixteenth and the nineteenth centuries. Thus, in a certain sense, European 'history' dialectically dictated 'the absence of history' in America for four centuries.

2. With regard to raw materials of vital necessity the USA was virtually the only self-sufficient imperialist power. Her oil resources, especially, were incomparably better than those of her rivals between 1871 and 1945, though after the Second World War the enormous extension of production and transportation in the United States ended this self-sufficiency. Today the USA is becoming increasingly dependent on foreign imports, especially from Latin America, of two raw materials – iron ore and oil.

ket. By 1913 she produced 40% of the world's steel, more than that of France, Great Britain and Germany together. By 1927 she had overtaken the whole of Europe and by 1949 had exceeded it by nearly 50%.

The two world wars only resulted in the mutual enfeeblement of the United States' main competitors. By 1945 the process outlined above seemed to have reached its zenith. Germany, Japan, Great Britain, France and Italy had lost practically all their autonomous military and economic power.

However, the United States has been unable to consolidate its absolute superiority for three reasons:

1. At the end of the First World War one great nation left the world imperialist system. Despite the decline of the international revolutionary movement after 1923, despite reaction and increasing bureaucratization in the USSR itself, the economic advances of the October Revolution were maintained. They permitted rapid economic development and the creation of a huge industry which, in the last analysis, explains the USSR's victorious resistance to the assaults of German imperialism during the Second World War. The Soviet Union, it is true, was incredibly weakened, bleeding and starving at the end of the war,[3] but her military capacity and more than that, her political influence, were too vividly appreciated by the populations of the victorious West for it to be possible for the USA purely and simply to eliminate her as a power factor.[4] The result, on the con-

3. According to official Soviet statistics (*The National Economy of the USSR Statistical Information*, Foreign Languages Press, Moscow, 1957), steel production in 1945 had fallen to 35% of that in 1940, oil to 40% and timber to 50%. The output of cement, textiles and tractors had fallen below the level of 1930 or even 1928.
4. Later analyses failed to take sufficient account of the important part played by agitation amongst American troops for their immediate repatriation at the end of the Japanese war (see Harry S. Truman, *Year of Decision*, Doubleday, New York, 1955, pp. 506–10).

trary, was the 'Cold War'; a world divided into spheres of influence, giving rise to the vast economic and military growth of the Eastern bloc. With the development of nuclear weapons by the Soviet Union, this finally reduced the American dream of global hegemony to ashes.

2. The decline of the old colonial empires during the Second World War was followed by violent revolutionary movements amongst the peoples of underdeveloped countries who had, until then, been the principal victims of capitalist imperialism. It seemed at first as though these movements were mainly directed against Western Europe and – to a lesser extent – Japan, and that America was destined to be their major beneficiary. In other words, they would allow her to establish an economic dominance in these former colonies similar to that which she already exercised in the formally independent but in fact semi-colonial Latin American states.

Cuba was the great turning-point. American imperialism was given a practical lesson in permanent revolution. That is to say, it was clearly shown that any mass movement for the liberation of a developing country from the political and economic hegemony of imperialist capital tends to break away from the imperialist world system and to start building a socialist economy. Otherwise no genuine anti-imperialist liberation is possible. This experience forced the American bourgeoisie to undertake a radical revision of its global strategy. Henceforward the object of its foreign policy was to prevent another Cuba, to eliminate any revolution which might become socialist, either by supporting military putsches (Brazil, Argentina, Indonesia, Ghana), or by intervening itself (Vietnam, Dominican Republic). This has already led, and will increasingly lead, to strategic revisions on an international scale in which Europe appears as the 'rear' of the American front against colonial revolution – a 'rear' which must be safeguarded by a policy of détente towards the Soviet Union. This means a further diminution of the area in which US power is supreme.

3. Confronting these two poles, the Eastern bloc and the colonial revolution, America's global strategy was finally forced to restore and support the economic strength of Western Europe and Japan. It is a commonplace to assert that the rebirth of West Germany and Japan after the Second World War was the fruit of the Cold War. This is undeniable. It is clear that in 1947–8 the United States decided to re-establish its European and Japanese competitors for fear that these countries might desert the capitalist camp.[5]

However, it should also be emphasized that the process which ended in putting West European and Japanese capitalism back on its feet was *not solely* an inevitable product of the Cold War (i.e. the pressure on America to give political and military support to its allies). It was also the result of *economic necessities* inherent in American capitalism. It is

5. Thus the condemnation of the Marshall Plan by the Stalinist-led communist parties on the grounds that this Plan and the economic integration of Europe were only designed to make Europe a political satellite and economic helot of the USA, proved completely ill-founded. (See, amongst others, E. Bregel, *Steuern, Anleihen und Inflation im Dienste des Imperialismus*, Verlag Die Wirtschaft, Berlin, 1955, pp. 182 *et seq.*) What happened was the opposite. The Marshall Plan and the economic integration of Europe marked the beginning of a new era of development of various European imperialist powers. They created the objective conditions for their increasing independence of the USA, and although it is true that they did not exercise this independence outside the sphere of the world imperialist alliance (and Gaullist France was no exception), this was not because they were prevented from doing so by the United States, but because their class interests demanded the Atlantic alliance. As for Japan, the United States began pushing for the 'restoration' of the economy as early as 1946, though their policy was riddled with contradictions; for differences among American capitalist groups see T. A. Bisson, *Zaibatsu Dissolution in Japan*, Berkeley, 1954, p. 42.

here that we can clearly recognize the effects of the law of unequal development applied to the United States itself.

After the Second World War and the end of the first post-war economic cycle, the American economy was structurally characterized by a constantly increasing surplus productive capacity and by a growing surplus of capital which it was no longer economic to invest under 'normal' conditions.[6] Equally typical was a fall in the rate of profit, chiefly the result of the disappearance of unemployment during the war, and a steep rise in wages and a consequent fall in the rate of surplus value.

This surplus capital was not held by the middle classes but was concentrated in the hands of the 'corporations' – oligopolistic companies which dominate the American economy.[7] This is the kind of situation in which one would

6. I have already described elsewhere, in *Marxist Economic Theory* (Monthly Review, New York, 1968), the post-war American economic cycle which led to the recessions of 1949, 1953, 1957 and 1960. The increasing frequency of these cycles by comparison with those before the war is a result of the increasing pace of technological innovation.

7. According to official American government estimates the figure by value added for the 200 largest US companies rose from 30% in 1947 to 38% in 1958 and to 41% in 1963; their contribution to new capital expenditure reached 46% of the total in 1963 (*USA Statistical Abstract 1968*, p. 731). In 1964 Gardner C. Means testified before the same committee that the hundred largest companies in manufacturing industry had by 1963 accumulated 50% of the fixed capital value (land, buildings, and equipment) of all the joint stock companies together (*New York Times*, 2 July 1964). According to the *Hearings before the Subcommittee on Antitrust and Monopoly of the Committee of the Judiciary* (88th Congress, 2nd session), the hundred largest American companies had increased their share in the total capital assets of all American companies from 41·3% to 49% between 1947 and 1962. Paul Huvelin (in *Les investissements étrangers en Europe*, ed. P. Uri, Éditions Dunod, Paris, 1967, p. 138) says 88% of money spent on research in America is invested by the two hundred largest corporations. In West Germany, factories employing more than 1,000 wage earners accounted for 34·3% of the aggregate industrial labour force in 1952, 38·8% in 1957, and 40·6% in 1966.

expect huge sums of capital to be exported but, except for those producing raw materials, it does not make sense for the big corporations to promote large-scale capital exports to the so-called Third World. The markets are too limited there, and the amortization of investments in costly installations is not adequately guaranteed politically and socially. This is why the big American companies have exported such enormous amounts of capital to Western Europe, Canada, and Japan. This had reached 50 billion dollars in 1965 and 60 billion in 1967, against 7·2 billions in 1949.[8] This explains why the returns from foreign investment, which only represented 10% of the profits of American companies in 1950, amounted to 24% of their gross profits by 1964.[9] But this gigantic transfusion of American capital was accompanied by an enormous infusion of American technology and 'know-how'. European industries which had been des-

8. *Survey of Current Business*, August 1964, p. 10. The figures for 1967 were calculated by the author. The figures for 1965 are those published by Niels Grosse in 'Amerikanische Direktinvestitionen in Europa', in *Europa Archiv*, 1, 1967. (Translator's note: the word billion is used throughout this text in the American sense of a thousand million.) In the period 1955–60 an average of 2·8 billion dollars a year was exported by private capitalists and corporations to underdeveloped countries, and an average of 2·7 billion dollars a year to other imperialist countries. By 1961–6 the balance had shifted sharply. The average annual export of private capital to underdeveloped countries was only 2·3 billion dollars whereas the annual average export of private capital to imperialist countries was 4·2 billion dollars. As for United States private capital alone, the flow to imperialist countries was already double the flow to underdeveloped countries from 1955–60 and three times the flow to underdeveloped countries from 1961–6. (These figures are taken from an article by Michael Barratt Brown, 'The Structure of the World Economy', written for the German Suhrkamp Encyclopedia.)

9. Harry Magdoff, in 'Problems of United States Capitalism', *The Socialist Register 1965*, ed. Ralph Miliband and John Saville, Monthly Review, New York, 1965. On a lesser scale an analogous process has occurred in Great Britain which has exported an annual average of £300 million over the last ten years. At the end of 1964 foreign investment by private individuals and companies had risen to £9·5 billion, equivalent to some 25 billion dollars.

troyed or were obsolescent at the end of the war were hence-
forth reconstructed along the most modern lines. This was
especially the case in those branches of industry which
underwent rapid expansion (consumer durables, chemicals,
plastics, synthetic materials and, to some extent, the
machine-tool industry) and in the iron and steel industry,
where the average age of machinery is now less than that of
its American counterpart. The factors which, until the early
1960s, caused the economies of Western Europe and Japan
to expand more rapidly than the American economy intensified this trend.[10]

Table 1

Production of crude iron (in millions of tons)

	1929	1946	1953	1966	1967
USA	57·3	61	101·3	124·7	118·1
The Six	35·6	11·8	39·7	85	90
Britain	9·8	12·9	17·9	24·7	24·2
Japan	3·8	2·0	9·8	47·4	62·1

These same inherently economic reasons explain the sensational comeback of Western Europe and Japan into the
world's markets. In 1947 Western Europe's share of international trade had fallen to under 34%, compared with 27%
for Canada and the United States. By 1965 Western
Europe's share had risen to over 40% compared with only
18% for North America. These figures are all the more sig-

10. For the causes of the 'economic miracle' in West Germany, France,
Italy and elsewhere see the author's 'The Economics of Neo-Capitalism' in
The Socialist Register 1965, ed. Ralph Miliband and John Saville, Monthly
Review, New York, 1964, and Theodor Prager, *Wirtschaftswunder oderkeines?*
Europa Verlag, Vienna, 1963.

nificant if one recalls that during the same period Japan's
and the Eastern bloc's share of world trade had considerably
increased, Japan's from less than 1% in 1947 and 2% in
1955 to 4·5% in 1965. In certain important sectors of industrial production Western Europe was rapidly able to
close the gap between itself and the USA resulting from the
Second World War, and in some cases to achieve a relative
improvement of its situation *vis-à-vis* America.

Table 2
Car production (in millions)

	1937	1950	1955	1966	1967
USA	3·9	6·7	7·9	8·6	7·4
The Six	0·5	0·6	1·5	6·1	5·7
Britain	0·4	0·5	0·9	1·6	1·5
Japan*	0·1	—	0·1†	2·2	3·1

* The figures for Japan include trucks, the figures for the other
countries do not.   † 1956.

Even more striking is what happens in a typically expanding sector – plastics:

Table 3
Production of plastics (in thousands of tons)

	1955	1965
USA	1,744·2	5,217·8
West Germany	355·2	1,953·2
The Six	595·5	3,893·0
Britain	323·4	973·0
Japan	101	1,603·0

Table 4

Exports of plastics (in thousands of tons)

	1955	1965
USA	131·6	535·4
West Germany	78·8	686·2
The Six	132·8	1529·8
Britain	85·6	338·8
Japan	5·4	253·9

Table 5

The export of machinery for the manufacture of rubber and plastic goods (in millions of dollars)

	1954	1958	1962
USA	21·3	30·8	55·0
West Germany	7·9	23·9	66·7
Britain	7·5	16·4	34·5

Of course, the significance of these figures should not be exaggerated. Foreign trade does not play such an important role in the American economy as it does in the economies of Japan and Western Europe, and there is still a considerable gap separating Western Europe and the United States in the production of goods and services (in 1965 the gross product of all the capitalist states of Europe was only 70% of that of the USA alone). While there can be no question that the United States has lost the absolute superiority it had in 1945, it has certainly not lost its relative superiority.

That this is so is shown by the economic, military and

political developments of recent years. It is precisely the dialectical relationship between the loss of the United States' absolute supremacy and the consolidation of her relative advance which still governs much of the course of the relations between the USA and Western Europe. An understanding of this dialectic is the key to an understanding of these relations. It is evident that neither this dialectic nor the causes of America's economic superiority can be explained by resorting to comparative national psychology or the 'pioneer spirit'.

Chapter 2

International Concentration of Capital

The principal forces behind the rapid expansion of the European economy between 1950 and 1964 were: the new industrial revolution, a pressing need to make up the vast gap in the production of consumer durables, a slowly re-emerging arms industry, and rapid industrialization – above all of underdeveloped areas – bordering on the economic heartland of Western Europe.[1] All these factors brought about a rapid expansion of the internal market and increasing exports of industrial goods. After a few years' delay, Japan experienced a similar development. The American economy, as well as that of the Eastern bloc, had to try and keep up with this expansion. Thus the world's economy now finds itself confronted with increasingly sharp competition on the world market which forces every nation to fight an ever tougher struggle to maintain, let alone extend, its share of rapidly increasing international trade.

1. This heartland consists of two triangles – Paris, Amsterdam, Munich; and Paris, Munich, Genoa. The real underdeveloped areas of the Common Market lie outside these triangles (e.g. Central and Southern Italy, South-West France and so on) as do, in a wider sense, the underdeveloped areas of Northern and Southern Europe.

The logical result of this sharpening international competition was an increasing international concentration and centralization of capital. In this context, the specific forms that govern the general tendencies of capitalist production within the framework of the world economy stand out in sharp relief. Starting with the hypothesis, which history corroborates, of limited international mobility of capital, Marx demonstrated that there is no single average rate of profit for the world markets, but that numerous average rates exist side by side: among other things, this enables the technologically more developed nations to produce surplus profits from trade with underdeveloped nations.[2]

But Marx, by contrast with Ricardo and his law of comparative costs, realized that this reduced mobility of capital was not an absolute law. Capital crosses frontiers, though the amounts involved are modest compared to those invested in the heart of the great capitalist empires. In the era of classical imperialism before the First World War, this capital flowed mainly into the colonies and semi-colonies dependent on the great powers. This led to a very special global division of labour in which the Third World specialized in the production of raw materials and foodstuffs for the imperialist nations, although even at that time a not inconsiderable amount of capital was invested in countries which were not strictly speaking colonial or semi-colonial. Thus, there was French and Belgian investment in Russia,

2. *Capital*, vol. 1, chap. 20. These surplus profits which Marx considered to be the product of the exchange of more productive and intensive labour against less productive and intensive labour, can result not only from traditional exchange of finished articles for raw materials, but also from the exchange of machinery and means of transport for the products of light industry, and even from the exchange of the products of a technologically more developed industry for those of a technologically less developed industry. This is the key to an understanding of international capital flows over the last twenty years.

German investment in Austro-Hungary, European – especially British – investment in the USA, and so forth.[3] This capital, too, was not only used for the traditional financing of railways, ports, sources of raw materials, and passive investment in the stock of foreign companies (portfolio investment – the typical form particularly of British capital investment in the USA). It also created a number of important manufacturing industries – notably the Russian iron and steel industry. However, this involved only a small fraction of total capital invested abroad and was rightly seen as only a secondary phenomenon of the international movement of capital.

The colossal transfusion of American capital into the German economy between the two world wars had the most catastrophic effects during the 1929–33 economic crisis. Even though it was then still mainly a question of loans to the public sector and short-term investments, and not so much of direct investments in industry, there were already cases of take-overs of important industrial companies such as that of Opel by General Motors.[4]

But it is only since the Second World War that the trend towards international centralization and concentration of capital has got under way at any speed, and it is no longer the underdeveloped countries which are the object of this process but the highly industrialized nations.[5] In order to

3. According to Professor A. J. Brown, *Introduction to the World Economy*, Allen and Unwin, London, 1966, p. 110, between 4 and 5% of American capital at the end of the nineteenth century belonged to foreigners.
4. For direct American investment in Europe before the Second World War see F. A. Southard's *American Industry in Europe*, Houghton Mifflin, Boston, 1931.
5. Immediately after the occupation of most of continental Europe by Nazi imperialism, German Capital started to appropriate the most important means of production in many occupied countries – a process which was only reversed when Germany suffered military defeat.

understand the process as a whole correctly, the various forms it takes must be carefully distinguished:

(a) There are cases when a 'national' industry suffers out-and-out 'alienation' in favour of a foreign country's capital. This is the logical result of a balance of forces which no longer permits the national bourgeoisie to use state power to protect its own interests against those of a foreign power. This process in part started to develop in West Germany and Japan after 1945, but subsequently came to an abrupt halt.[6] If it is pushed to its bitter end, a once independent imperialist power can be transformed into a semi-colony like Brazil or Greece.

(b) If the process is arrested in its initial stages so that only certain sectors of the economy fall under foreign control, the situation can be described as foreign capital pene-

6. The absorption of the Phoenix Werke, Hamburg-Harburg by the American Firestone consortium is a good example of appropriation under favourable political circumstances. At the end of 1964 the German Federal Bank estimated the total of foreign capital in the West Germany economy at almost 3 billion dollars – which corresponded to just over 15% of all capital invested in non-agricultural industries. This should be compared to the 6 billion Reichsmarks which the League of Nations estimated was the value of foreign investment in the whole of Germany in the middle of 1931. However, in the motor industry, in office machinery and in the petroleum industry the percentage is much higher, and nearly half of the foreign-owned capital is in American hands. In addition, the Federal Republic has witnessed mergers comparable to that of Machines Bull with General Electric in France. The Kuba Imperial radio and television company was bought by General Electric, and Reiwerke (a major detergent manufacturer) was taken over by the US firm of Procter and Gamble. Recently the American Gillette trust bought out Braun and it now holds 85% of the stock of this manufacturer of high quality electrical appliances, an operation which cost it about 200 million marks.

In a recent study published by the Italian National Council of Industry and Labour it was estimated that 14% of Italian industry was foreign-owned. Just over a third of foreign investment in Italy was owned by Americans, who controlled 5·7% of Italian industrial capital. One in four large Italian companies is foreign-owned, and one in eight is American-owned.

tration – a state of affairs in which there is no qualitative change in politico-economic relations. This is the position of American capital penetration into most European economies, although the strategic importance of the sectors controlled by US capital – petroleum, computers, and sometimes petro-chemicals, tyres, telecommunications and aircraft – extend well beyond its relatively modest share of total capital outlay.[7] Thus, a study by the European Economic Commission revealed that in 1965 80% of Common Market computer production, 24% of the motor industry, 15% of the synthetic rubber industry, and 10% of the production of petro-chemicals was under the management of American subsidiaries.[8] Even in a country as rich in

7. A series of articles has been published by Francesco Magistrelli and Guglielmo Ragozzino on American investment in the Common Market which support these conclusions (*Problemi del Socialismo*, November–December 1965 and July–August 1966). The annual sum invested in the Common Market by American companies or their subsidiaries rose from 228 million dollars in 1958 to 908 million dollars in 1965. The sum total of these investments for the eight years in question amounted to nearly 5 billion-dollars, and a grand total of 7·5 billion dollars has been estimated as the sum of all American investment in Western Europe, private investment included. The Chairman of the Administrative Committee of the Union des Banques Suisses calculated the total value of American investment in Europe in 1966 to be 17·5 billion dollars. 69% was direct investment, 16% was held in the form of stocks and bonds and 15% was in bank deposits. European investment in the USA is reckoned to be 17·8 billion dollars, but only 32% of that is in private investment (see Jean Meynaud and Dušan Sidjanski, *L'Europe des Affaires*, Éditions Payot, Paris, 1967, p. 75). Between 1958 and 1963, over 3,000 American companies either set up subsidiaries in the EEC or gained control over already existing firms within it.

8. European competition, too, can tend to the 'alienation' of national industries when foreign firms are established in a country without significant participation by domestic capital. In the Common Market this trend is especially marked in light industry. Meynaud and Sidjanski (op. cit., pp. 20, 25) cite several cases of this in foodstuffs, clothing and textiles.

The share of direct American investment in gross capital formation within the Common Market rose from 4·5% in 1958 to 6·3% in 1964, but it reached

capital as Switzerland, American investment is widespread
– in 1950 it was 25 million dollars, in 1963 it was 670
million dollars, in 1964 948 million, in 1965 1,116 million
and by 1966 it had risen to 1,210 million dollars. The number of subsidiaries of American companies in Switzerland
has grown from about fifty before the Second World War to
some four hundred in 1955 and 640 by the end of 1966.[9] It
is interesting to note that 40% of all US direct investment
in Britain, Germany and France is owned by the three giant
corporations – General Motors, Ford and Standard Oil of
New Jersey (Esso).

(c) But if, instead of dominant penetration by a single
nation in other industrial nations, there is increasing foundation or absorption of companies by capital from various
nations, without any one of them holding a position of
hegemony, we are no longer confronted with one imperialist
power dominating one or many national economies, but
with a new phenomenon: the international interpenetration
of capital.

(d) Finally, capital concentration and centralization can
be limited to 'national capital' – i.e. it can occur in the classical form described in economic literature.

As we suggested above, we can provisionally leave the
first hypothesis aside, at least in so far as it concerns West-

---

10% in Italy and the Benelux countries. In Great Britain, the share of Ameri-
can subsidiaries in annual investment in manufacturing industry is of the
order of 16% (Fernand Braun, in *Les investissements étrangers en Europe*, ed.
Pierre Uri and others, Éditions Dunod, Paris, 1967, p. 189; Niels Grosse,
'Amerikanische Direktinvestitionen in Europa' in *Europa Archiv*, 1, 1967;
Meynaud and Sidjanski, op. cit.)

9. *Le Monde*, 30 April 1968. Swiss companies such as Raffineries du
Rhône, Stoffel in St Gallen and La Schape in Geneva (textiles), Buren and
Universal-Genève (watches) have recently been absorbed by American
companies.

ern Europe, since none of the industrialized nations there is currently being taken over wholesale by American Capital.[10] But the concentration and centralization of capital caused by the present bitter international competition do take the three other forms mentioned, at least in West Europe. These can be illustrated by three examples involving major corporations.

The absorption of Machines Bull (of France) and of the electronic computer section of the Italian firm of Olivetti by the American General Electric trust is an example of international capital concentration favouring American overall supremacy.

The merger of the two giants of the European photographic industry, Gevaert of Belgium and Agfa of Western Germany, or the new steel combine made up between Hoogovens Ijmuiden of Holland, Dortmund Horder Hütten Union and Hoesch of West Germany, are examples of the international interpenetration of capital without any particular nation predominating.

The merger of the two great Italian chemical trusts,

10. It is true that there is an exception: Canada, a modern industrial nation where ownership of an absolute majority of the non-agricultural means of production has fallen to the USA (see A. E. Safarian, *Foreign Ownership of Canadian Industry*, McGraw-Hill, Toronto, 1966). The case of Spain is interesting too. In the last decade it has become a playground for foreign capital; however, a skilful policy of playing-off American, French, British, West German and even Japanese interests against each other has hindered or prevented the dominance of any one great power. The total capital invested in Spain in the last five years has been nearly a billion dollars of which, however, between a quarter and a third has been spent on land or real estate. Of the three hundred largest American companies, 173 have subsidiaries in Spain with the participation of Spanish capital (Arturo Lopez Muñoz and José Garcia Delgado, *Crecimiento y crisis del capitalismo español*, Cuadernos Para el Dialogo, Madrid, 1968, pp. 165–7, 170–7). A recent plan to build a petrol refinery at Bilbao saw the emergence of five competing consortiums: Franco-British, Anglo-Spanish, Spanish-American, Spanish, and Italian-Spanish-American (*Financial Times*, 29 July 1968).

Edison and Montecatini, joined later by the chemical section of the state trust ENI; the merger of three French steel companies, de Wendel, Sidélor and Mosellane de Sidérurgie; and the merger of Thyssen and Hüttenwerke Oberhausen in West Germany (followed by a cooperative agreement with another West German steel giant, Mannesmann) are all examples of capital concentration at a national level brought about by international competition.

American economists, businessmen and politicians try to conceal the differences between the first and second forms of capital concentration by referring to multinational corporations. In *Monopoly Capital*, Baran and Sweezy attribute the first use of the term 'multinational corporation' to David E. Lilienthal.[11] In a recent speech in Brussels, Jacques Maisonrouge, president of the American IBM trust in Europe, expressed the wish that multinational corporations should operate with multinational capital but leave the direction of their subsidiaries in different countries to the citizens of those countries.[12]

But the concept of multinationality used here is merely formal. IBM, Standard Oil of New Jersey, and General Motors may be multinational in the sense that their shares are quoted on the stock exchange in many countries and their subsidiaries cover most of the world (Standard Oil sells its products in more than a hundred countries and controls 175 subsidiary companies in 52 of them). Many of these subsidiary companies are managed by the nationals of the country in which the company is working and sometimes the majority of profits even comes from abroad (though this does *not* apply in the case of most American

11. Paul A. Baran and Paul M. Sweezy, *Monopoly Capital*, Monthly Review, New York, 1966, p. 193n.
12. *L'Echo de la Bourse* (Brussels), 11 October 1966.

oligopolistic trusts).[13] But there is not the least doubt that all the corporations are controlled by quite specific American financial bodies (in this case, the Watson family with the Morgans in the background, and the Rockefeller and Du Pont de Nemours groups).[14]

The European bourgeoisie, needless to say, is acutely concerned by the question whether control of its major productive plants lies on its side of the Atlantic or the other side. Not that it is guided in business matters by ethical or national considerations. Its motherland is where it can accumulate capital. Not only has a cheque no smell, it is also unencumbered by national frontiers.

But even if men can fly to the moon, it is still a long way across the Atlantic. Capital controlled from the other side can be devalued, or confiscated, from one day to the next. If European capitalists had half their capital invested on the other side and thus established a real international 'distribution of risk', they could forget about European nationalism (let alone petty intra-European nationalism). Unluckily for them, however, the American concept of multinationality is not founded on complete reciprocity.

---

13. Examples include Socony Mobil Oil, National Cash Register, Singer Sewing Machines, and Burroughs. The overseas contribution to profits is from 30 to 50% in Eastman Kodak, Caterpillar Tractor, International Harvester, Corn Products, Minnesota Mining and Manufacturing (the 3 M). There are equally some European corporations which have no difficulty in earning the majority of their profits from foreign investment, such as Bayer (with 62·1% of its business abroad), Hoesch, Philips, British Oxygen, etc.
14. Professor Jacques Houssiaux has given a subtle and detailed analysis of the concept of 'multi-national corporations' in *L'entreprise et l'économie au XXᵉ siecle*, ed. F. Bloch-Laîné and François Perroux, Presse Universitaire de France, Paris, 1966, vol. I, pp. 291–328. We believe, however, that the facts speak even clearer than this analysis, and that both corporations like IBM and General Motors, as well as more tightly centralized ones like Du Pont, are in the last analysis remote-controlled by 'decisive' financial interests in the United States – at least in so far as supreme decisions of economic strategy are concerned.

Accordingly, for West European capitalists, the loss of capital invested in West Europe still means the loss of their main fortune, if not their utter ruin. Therefore, to secure and defend their capital they need a state power of their own, and they need control over this capital in order to be able to control their state. The result is that their instinct for survival alone dictates that they must resist the excessive control of their means of production by their transatlantic friends.[15]

'Super-Imperialism' is still beyond the horizon. The decisive strata of West European capitalism are therefore not indifferent towards the three possible forms of international concentration of capital, though this naturally does not exclude the existence of certain groups which have tied their fate to American concerns and express this economic link through the ideology of 'Atlantic Union'. Confronted by the choice between 'national capital concentration' and 'international interpenetration of capital' these decisive strata will act according to their calculation of what will increase their ability to compete on the world market – that is, in the first place, against US capital (and, probably tomorrow, against Japanese capital).

International competition is itself the essential driving force behind the international concentration of capital. The oligopolistic trusts controlling a national market have a large capital surplus because of their excess monopoly profits which they cannot invest at home without upsetting

15. The significant word is 'excessive'. No responsible representative of West European capital, not even De Gaulle, has expressed himself as fundamentally opposed to *all* American capital investment in West Europe. That would be against the interests of the European bourgeoisie because Europe would thereby shut herself off from technical progress and the American monopoly of 'know-how' would be strengthened (see J.-J. Servan-Schreiber, *The American Challenge*, Atheneum, New York, 1968).

the monopolistic structure of their own market. They are thus driven towards international expansion by three motives.

The first is the aim of outdoing a domestic competitor by enlarging the scale of their operations and achieving sufficient power on a global scale to be able forcibly to modify returns which may still be unfavourable to them at home. The expansion of the computer branch of General Electric into Europe by the take-over of Machines Bull and Olivetti computers was just such a move in competition with IBM.

The second aim is to acquire an international range of operations not possible at home, as the only way of competing effectively with foreign companies. Péchiney, for example, produces 450,000 tons of aluminium in France. On the French market, it cannot rival its main competitors, ALCOA of the USA (producing a million tons), ALCAN of Canada (producing another million tons), or Reynolds and Kaiser, both of the USA (producing 800,000 tons); hence, it tries to establish factories in the United States, West Germany, and Japan.

Finally, a third aim may be to absorb a foreign competitor in order to prevent it from disturbing the monopolistic structure of the international market, or to build up defences against other foreign competitors. The Agfa–Gevaert merger and the Fiat–Citroën association correspond to this pattern.

Stephen Hymer, therefore, is absolutely correct in attacking the marginalist theory according to which international capital movements only occur in response to differences in the rates of profitability and interest – that capital moves from countries where it is in excess to countries where it is scarce. He is also correct in evoking the influence of 'oligopolistic strategy' and attempts 'to maximize profits on a world scale'.[16] But he is incorrect in neglecting the importance of the influence of varying national wage rates, the cost of fuel and raw materials, and local productivity on this 'maximization': in other words, the different rates of profitability in different countries. True, this is not a factor of decisive importance, but it is one which still plays an important part in monopoly strategy.[17]

16. Stephen Hymer, 'Direct Foreign Investment and International Oligopoly' (an article completed in June 1965 at Yale and discussed in a seminar at the Law Faculty of the Sorbonne in 1968).
17. For further details of the effect technological progress and the minimum profitable plant size have on the trend towards capital concentration see the beginning of Chapter 4.

Chapter 3

The Relative Superiority
of American Firms

In international competition the United States still commands a relative superiority over Western Europe. This reflects her ability to produce at lower unit costs despite higher wages. Higher American productivity has two roots: size (above all in the amount of capital) and technological advance.

Much has been written about the differences in the size of American and European industries – the origin of crucial economies of scale for American trusts. Consider, for example, the following statistics from a report prepared by UNICE, the European Community Industrial Union, the EEC's employers' federation:

In 1964 of the hundred largest businesses in the capitalist world, sixty-five were American, eighteen belonged to the EEC, eleven were British, and five were Japanese.

The largest motor manufacturer in the EEC (Volkswagen) made only a fifth of the number of cars produced by the largest American automobile manufacturer – this despite the fact that car production in the EEC had risen to 70% of that in the USA.

The turnover of the twenty largest American corporations almost equals the gross national product of West Germany, and the turnover of the five largest American corporations is almost the same as the gross national product of Italy.

Of the five hundred largest businesses in the capitalist world, the largest in the EEC, Philips, is only thirty-third. Volkswagen – the biggest German company – is thirty-fourth. The biggest French corporation, Rhône-Poulenc, is fourty-fourth, and the biggest Belgian company, Petrofina, is a hundred and fortieth.

The turnover of General Motors is equal to the sum total of the turnover of the thirteen largest German companies.[1]

It should also be emphasized (still according to the EEC employers' data) that American businesses are not only larger than their European counterparts but the process of capital concentration is proceeding much more rapidly in the USA than in the EEC. In the United States between 1954 and 1958, 4,400 mergers were registered, whereas in the first four years of the EEC's existence (1958–62) there were barely more than a thousand.[2]

The enormously greater size of the American monopolies is the reason why their rates of profit are so much higher, their volume of profits is larger, and therefore why they are more self-financing. European companies tend to be deeper in debt than American companies which in turn increases the gap between their respective rates of profit.

Naturally, publications like that just quoted and others of the same kind, are designed as special pleading by UNICE and other employers' federations. Not that they

1. For a comparison made in the 1950s see Joe S. Bain, *International Differences in Industrial Structure*, Yale University Press, New Haven, 1966.

2. Although there has recently been a spectacular increase in mergers in the UK (*The Times*, 29 January 1969); connected with this is the enormous increase in the role of American banks in Britain (*Financial Times*, 4 June 1968).

are trying to foster 'European nationalism'; they are merely aiming to cushion or eliminate paragraphs in the Treaty of Rome which hinder the concentration of capital and economic power, where these could mean control of the market.[3] Big Capital brings constant pressure to bear on the EEC Commission to apply these paragraphs with the greatest restraint or not at all, and there can be little doubt that the EEC officials will increasingly give way to this pressure.

The chemical industry offers a good illustration of the great advantages American firms draw from their larger financial resources, higher profit rates, greater self-financing capacity, superior access to the money market, and ability to purchase expensive modern equipment. For despite the fact that this is a branch of industry where research is of the utmost importance and has been conducted with success in Europe (at least in West Germany and Great Britain), American companies have cornered 41% of the world's trade (the Eastern bloc included), compared with only 20·5% for the EEC. Furthermore, the Americans employ only 880,000 people in this sector as against a million in the EEC so that the financial turnover for each American employee is 2·25 times larger than for his European counterpart.

It is true that research and development costs by the EEC chemical industry do not even amount to a third of what the Americans spend in this field. As for net profits: those of the major American trusts are more than 8%

3. Article 86 of the Treaty of Rome only provides for sanctions against firms which *abuse* their privileged position in the market, and only when such abuse affects trade between member states. On the other hand, Article 66 of the Treaty which established the European Coal and Steel Community, provides for sanctions against any company dominating the market which might impede genuine competition and lead to socio-economic consequences in conflict with the aims of the Coal and Steel Community.

of their turnover, whilst those of their major European rivals are only about 4%. It is significant, too, that in 1965 25% of the American chemical industry's net investment was made abroad and that these investments abroad alone were greater than *all* British and German investments in this field.

The greater size of American enterprises and their greater financial power are the most important factors behind the technological advantage they have recently gained. They can afford far larger research and development costs than their European rivals. But this is not the only reason why the Americans have taken the technological lead. Two other factors play an important part: America's gigantic military expenditure, and the emigration of the best European scientists to the USA.

The permanent arms economy which has prevailed in the USA virtually since 1940 obviously accounts for many of the changes in American capitalism.[4]

---

4. The effects of the arms race on the American economy has provoked a prolific literature. The following are some of the more relevant works: Fred J. Cook, 'Juggernaut, the Warfare State', in a special number of *The Nation*, 20 October 1961; C. Wright Mills, *The Power Elite* (Chapter 9), Oxford University Press, New York, 1956; P. A. Baran and Paul M. Sweezy, *Monopoly Capital* (Chapter 7), Monthly Review, New York, 1966; Theodor Prager, *Wirtschaftswunder oder keines?* (Chapter 8), Europa Verlag, Vienna, 1963; Fritz Vilmar, *Rüstung und Abrüstung im Spätkapitalismus*, Europäische Verlagsanstalt, Frankfurt / M., 1965; Michael Kidron, *Western Capitalism since the War*, Weidenfeld and Nicolson, London, 1968.

In this context it is worth recalling that Trotsky made a masterly forecast of the militarization of the USA, almost to the exact date of its appearance. In a speech on 18 January 1926 he said: 'If the United States continues to advance over the next fifteen years she will do so at Europe's expense. . . . And what if she encounters obstacles braking her progress? There will be an unlimited spiral in American militarism, because the thwarted economic forces are bound to try and find such outlets.' This militarism developed in 1940, fourteen years after Trotsky's speech, following the restrictions which the economic crisis of 1928–33 and the widespread return to protectionism

One of the most important results of this permanent arms competition with a *non-capitalist* bloc is that, contrary to what happened during the inter-imperialist rivalry of the past, the Soviet Union is not compelled to get maximum use from the capital invested in the arms economy. Invention and scientific discovery, the technological revolution and industrial innovation, have almost been synchronized in that country.[5]

Not the least consequence of the continual arms race with a non-capitalist power is that American capitalism has been obliged, for the sake of self-preservation, to maintain an equivalent rate of technical progress in it, without caring whether capital invested in previous techniques has already been sufficiently exploited. This increasing abstraction from the problem of the maximum utilization of capital (or, in other words, this increasing socialization of the costs of capital investment in the arms economy, despite the con-

---

had imposed on the 'peaceful' expansion of American imperialism. The solid 'peaceful' reputation enjoyed by the USA at that time must be remembered in order to appreciate how inspired and remarkable this forecast of Trotsky's was. It should be contrasted with the monumental blunder of a bourgeois – though serious – economist, Josef Schumpeter, who 'demonstrated' the falsity of the Marxist theory of imperialism by claiming that the capitalist country *par excellence*, the United States, had not the slightest imperialist inclinations (Josef Schumpeter, *Imperialism and Social Classes*, Augustus Kelly, New York, 1951).

5. We say *almost* synchronized. In a perfect model of a socialized society there would be complete synchronization. But the Soviet economy is not such a perfect model, but a bureaucratically distorted (as Lenin would have said) or (as Trotsky or Oskar Lange have said) a bureaucratically degenerated one. This is the source of those contradictions which would not have been found in the perfect model. Thus the system of planning and direction of Soviet industry, both in Stalin's time and today, induces factory managers to have a built-in material interest in the *slowing down* of technological improvement. Soviet economists are fully aware of this (see E. Mandel, 'Le réforme de la planification soviétique et ses implications', in *Les Temps Modernes*, June 1965).

tinued existence of private property and private profit) by no means extends to the so-called civilian sector of industry – to the capitalist economy as a whole. Nuclear energy provides a good example of the great extent to which the problem of the full valorization of invested capital delays technical development in the USA which, despite its lead of several years in the military uses of nuclear power, still only ranks third in its exploitation for peaceful purposes. However, scientific discovery and technical improvement – the by-products of military research and the permanent arms economy – are bound to benefit the civilian economy, especially in chemicals and electronics.

Jean-Jacques Servan-Schreiber has published the following table showing the lag between scientific discoveries and industrial exploitation:[6]

112 years for photography (1727–1839)
56 years for the telephone (1829–1876)
35 years for the wireless (1867–1902)
15 years for radar (1925–1940)
6 years for the atom bomb (1939–1945)
5 years for the transistor (1948–1953)
3 years for the printed circuit (1958–1961)

Furthermore, the permanent arms economy in the USA involves the state in making far bigger contributions to financing research and development. The journal *Patronat Français* estimates this contribution at 64% in the USA, against 40% in West Germany, 37% in Belgium, and 3% in Holland. Of course, state contributions are significantly

6. Jean-Jacques Servan-Schreiber, *Le Défi American*, Éditions Denoël, Paris, 1967; Eng. tr., *The American Challenge*, Atheneum, New York, 1968, p. 67.

higher in the two West European countries which produce nuclear weapons – 64% in Great Britain and 69% in France.[7]

Thus American concerns enjoy a double advantage over their European rivals: they have more to spend on research because they are richer; and they receive bigger state subsidies for this research. This accounts for the technological lead they have taken in such areas as computers, lasers, and scientific instruments (the latter perhaps even more important than the technological gap in the computer industry).

At the National Conference on Social Welfare held at the beginning of April 1967, Professor Titmuss and Lord Bowden expressed their concern over the flight of scientists to the United States.[8] Titmuss estimates that about 100,000 first-class doctors, scientists and technicians have left for the USA since 1949, and that this represents a saving in training costs to the United States of four billion dollars and an equivalent loss for the rest of the world. About 20% of the annual increase in the number of doctors in the USA is accounted for by doctors trained abroad.[9] Britain alone has lost ten per cent of its doctors, engineers

7. *Patronat Français*, November 1965.
8. Lord Bowden, 'Inflation scientifique et fuite des cerveaux', *Les Temps Modernes*, May–June 1968.
9. This flow of West European scientists, doctors and top technicians to the USA naturally constitutes by no means the whole of this international centralization of 'educational capital'. At the same time – so to speak, as 'compensation' – there is a parallel flow of African and Asian graduates to West Europe, mainly to France and Great Britain. In Britain an increasing number of posts in the National Health Service are taken by Indian, African and West Indian doctors (the number of nurses from the Commonwealth is even larger), while an increasing number of British doctors emigrate to the United States. More doctors come from the extremely poor country of Togo to France than are sent from France to Togo.

and technologists to the USA in recent years. The EEC Commission estimates the loss for member countries at fifteen per cent. These figures naturally much underrate America's real gain and Europe's real loss for to the saving on the cost in training should be added the value of the resulting increase in research.[10] The reasons for this drain are the higher salaries and better working conditions America offers scientists, doctors and technicians.[11] But its inherent rationale leads to a typical process of concentration of profits, capital and wealth. By appropriating the educational 'capital' of other countries, the USA saves its own capital, so that instead of investing it in new schools, it can be used to finance new laboratories and research centres. This increases the American economy's technological lead, brings surplus profits to American business, and enables it to pay its research workers even more, which in turn leads to a further increase in the emigration of Western European scientists and to further saving of educational 'capital' in the USA.

The statistics bear this out. In 1962, 93·7 dollars per

10. According to Baran and Sweezy, op. cit., pp. 102–3, in the United States the expenditure on research and development by non-financial corporations rose from 3·5 billion dollars to 12 billion dollars between 1953 and 1962. If these figures are compared with expenditure on machinery and equipment, they have risen from 15% to 37% in this time. Moreover, to these figures should be added the expenditure by the public sector which over the last ten years has amounted to 3·4 to 5 billion dollars annually. Calculated thus, the total expenditure on research works out at about half that on machinery and equipment. It is not unreasonable for economists to conclude that technical progress lies at the root of the increase in the United States' gross national product by nearly 50% (in terms of fixed value) in the last six years.

11. One of America's best known talent scouts, William Douglas, recently described the 'brain drain' as an example of the triumph of mind over matter. However, he also declared that the main reason for the flight of scientists to the USA is higher pay. Thus, this idealist apologist for the American system seems to think that the key to scientists' minds is hard cash.

capita was spent on research in the USA, compared with 33·5 dollars in Britain and only 20 in the EEC. In the same year, 10·4 per thousand employees in the USA were engaged in research, compared with 6·1 in Britain and less than 4 in the EEC. In 1965 total expenditure on research and development in the United States amounted to 13·4 billion dollars, as against only 5·8 billion in Western Europe (including Britain, Sweden and Switzerland). Of course, these statistics should be interpreted with caution. Materials and labour cost less in Europe so that a dollar there will buy more than a dollar in the United States. But the qualitative difference becomes clear if expenditure on research is related to the gross national product. In 1963–4 in the USA it was 3·3% of the gross national product compared with an average of 1·5% in Europe. Moreover, the increasing number of American subsidiaries in European industry only widens the technological gap, for the great American corporations naturally tend to keep the lion's share of research expenditure for the mother company.

This increasing gap in the development of technology between Europe and America cannot simply be added to the disparities in size of the industries (which partly created it). The two factors act on each other and multiply the advantages which accrue to American concerns in international competition. This becomes all the clearer if it is recalled that, as a result of their more advanced technology, the much wealthier American concerns have reached a quite different phase in the organic composition of their capital,[12]

---

12. In Marxist economic theory the organic composition of capital is the relationship between constant capital (i.e. the value of raw materials, machinery, equipment, and buildings, etc., which goes into the value of the product) on the one hand, and the total sum of capital spent in producing that product on the other, which, besides the constant value, also comprises the variable value; in other words, the cost of paying for the labour employed in

which enables them to spend a comparatively smaller fraction of their capital on salaries and wages and a larger portion on machinery, equipment, and laboratories. The upshot is another vicious circle of international centralization of capital of which European firms are the victims and US concerns the beneficiaries.

It is this vicious circle which accounts for the surplus profits[13] of American concerns deriving from US technological monopoly, and explains why American concerns in Europe can both earn higher profits than at home and than West European concerns can themselves.[14] It also explains why US concerns can so easily obtain sufficient funds on

---

its production. Through competition, capital which has a higher organic composition wins a greater share of the overall surplus value than capital with lower organic composition (see Claude Evain in *Les investissements étrangers en Europe*, ed. Pierre Uri and others, Éditions Dunod, Paris, 1967, p. 248, who quotes a French industrial magnate as saying that his main American rival uses four times as much capital as he does but realizes forty times as much profit).

13. According to Servan-Schreiber the price of licences and patents for computers amounts to more than 15% of the turnover of their manufacture. According to the *OECD Observer* of April 1968, the USA is receiving more than 50% of all patent rights the world over, Britain receives 13% and West Germany 8%.

14. Baran and Sweezy, op. cit., pp. 198 *et seq.*, quote a special report in the weekly *US News and World Report* (1 June 1964) which summarizes a survey carried out amongst major US industralists thus: 'Profit rates abroad generally are higher than those in similar activities in the US. Many firms report a percentage return "twice as high abroad as in America".' *Business Week*, 20 April 1963, had a similar report. Heinz-Dieter Meier, who has devoted an M.A. thesis at the Free University of Berlin to a comparison between Servan-Schreiber's and my own analysis of European and American competition, has assembled empirical data which bear this out. Whereas the rate of profit of 35 big corporations in their US operations was 9·2% in 1960, it reached 14·2% in their foreign operations. According to the US Department of Commerce, net profit rates on American investments in Europe declined from 19% in 1955 to 13% in 1964, but remained substantially higher than net profit rates in manufacturing industry in the USA up to the mid-sixties (which were 15% in 1955, 10% in 1959, and 12% in 1962).

the European capital market to finance their expansion into Europe. Between 1962 and 1966 the branches of American corporations in Europe invested 22·5 billion dollars – 2·2 billion dollars through local self-financing, 5·5 billion through depreciation, and 9 billion through loans from the European capital market or through credits arranged with European banks. American capitalists, therefore, provided only a little more than a quarter of the investment capital. All Ford's subsidiaries in Europe actually managed to finance the whole of their investment with European capital.[15]

European directors and bankers, EEC officials and national governments are all fully aware of this situation. They know that it is vital for them to establish larger companies, to confront constantly intensifying international competition. Everyone – professional associations, national and international employers' associations, economists, politicians, ministers and EEC dignatories – all implore industrialists to merge. But the question remains: can business mergers on a national scale produce giants comparable to the great American corporations? Economic logic says no, for obvious reasons.

In *The American Challenge*, that adroit popularization of the views of capitalist circles in favour of 'European companies', Jean-Jacques Servan-Schreiber quotes Robert McNamara, the former American Secretary of Defence, to show that 'the technological gap is not so much a technological gap as it is a managerial gap'. 'The brain drain,' says McNamara, 'occurs not merely because we have more advanced technology here in the United States but rather

---

15. See Paul Einzig's *Foreign Dollar Loans in Europe*, St. Martin's, New York, 1965. The total issue of Eurobonds has risen from $346 million in 1963 to $1·4 billion in 1966, $1·86 billion in 1967, and $1·66 in the first half of 1968.

because we have more modern and effective management.'[16]
There are, however, numerous contradictions in this argument and even Servan-Schreiber's own book provides the
facts with which to refute his thesis.

It is significant that the majority of major discoveries on
the threshold of the third industrial revolution were made
by European and not American scientists. This is not only
true of splitting the atom. The first punched card system
and the mechanical processing of information were also
launched in Europe – in the middle of the Second World
War in Germany. Europe is not short of brains. In the
field of industrial innovation, too, Europe was by no means
behind the USA. England used nuclear energy in industry
before the USA, and European companies started the sale
of computers at the same time as the Americans, in 1953
when there were two American, two British, one French
and one West German company making electronic computers. In 1967 the Westinghouse Corporation attempted
to siphon off British scientists building the Dounreay prototype fast reactor which promised to have important sales in
the 1970s, further proof that the Americans were not leading in this field.[17] We should also note that Western Germany, too, has started to export nuclear power stations – the
first to Argentina in 1968 – and her fast reactors which will
be mass-produced in ten years' time promise to be the
geese which will lay the golden eggs of the 1980s. Competition between West Germany and the USA will be

16. Servan-Schreiber, op. cit., pp. 40, 75, 76, 83, and 158. John Diebold,
the American computer expert, supports McNamara's views, but pinpoints
the 'managerial' problem by pointing out that Europe lacks above all
middle-grade personnel able to analyse punched tape. The United States
already has 156,000 of these and should have 470,000 by 1970 (*Le Monde*,
15/16 October 1967).

17. *The Economist*, 18 November 1967, and *The Sunday Times*, 19 November 1967.

intensified in this field in the coming years.[18] Even in the area of scientific instruments where the American lead is considerable (65% of the total output of the major capitalist states in 1965), the annual growth rate between 1960 and 1965 has been 12·4% in West Germany, 13·8% in Japan, 23·5% in Great Britain, 34·5% in Sweden, and only 6·5% in the USA. By 1966 the total exports of America's seven major rivals, Germany, Japan, Great Britain, Sweden, France, Italy and Belgium, already exceeded that of the USA.

The lead which the American corporations have taken in the computer industry is a product of their greater capital resources and higher profits. These enable them to take greater risks, which is precisely what vanguard technology requires. (The IBM Corporation had to sink 5 billion dollars in four years into the building of its latest series of computers without being sure of realizing a profit on the investment. What European company could have taken such a risk?) Even if American laboratories fall behind they can afford to buy patents, ideas and technologists.[19] If any more help is needed there is the state-guaranteed profit from arms manufacture.

The supremacy of the USA is to be explained by the laws which Marx revealed a hundred years ago, the laws of the competition, accumulation, and concentration of capital –

18. *L'Echo de la Bourse* (Brussels), 13/14 October 1968; 27 August 1969.
19. A large number of inventions and technical innovations are still made in medium-size businesses in the USA. They act as testing grounds, as Rosa Luxemburg explained fifty years ago. These companies are only taken over by the monopoly corporations after success has been guaranteed. The Dutch professor, Kistemaker, the father of the technique of ultracentrifugation, has stressed the crucial role of these businesses in the progress of the United States, especially in the field of scientific instruments (*Het Parool*, 30 November 1968).

not some vague 'spiritual' force. So if it is not wrong to speak of 'the innovation gap', it is only in the specific sense that, although West European capitalism certainly has the intellectual and technical means, it very seldom has the financial resources for seizing the lead in industrial innovation.[20]

20. There is an exhaustive bibliography on this subject in the article by Klaus-Heinrich Standke in *Europa Archiv*, no. 16, 1967, which considers the 'technological gap' between Europe and the USA at length. Also of particular relevance is C. Freeman and A. Young, *The Research and Development Effort in Western Europe, North America and the Soviet Union*, OECD, Paris, 1965.

Chapter 4

Interpenetration of Capital in the EEC

Competition dictates the centralization of capital. European industrialists behave as Marx predicted.[1] The pressure in favour of the interpenetration of capital in Europe far surpasses that working for its national concentration.

Certain sectors of industry demand such intensive investment to attain profitable production that even all the companies in that sector in each individual Common Market country together cannot provide it. In such cases

---

1. 'Here competition rages in direct proportion to the number, and in inverse proportion to the magnitudes, of the antagonistic capitals. It always ends in the ruin of many small capitalists, whose capitals partly pass into the hands of their conquerors, partly vanish. Apart from this, with capitalist production an altogether new force comes into play – the credit system, which in its first stages furtively creeps in as the humble assistant of accumulation, drawing into the hands of individual or associated capitalists, by invisible threads, the money resources which lie scattered, over the surface of society, in larger or smaller amounts; but it soon becomes a new and terrible weapon in the battle of competition and is finally transformed into an enormous social mechanism for the centralization of capitals.

'Commensurately with the development of capitalist production and accumulation there develop the two most powerful levers of centralization – competition and credit' (*Capital*, Lawrence and Wishart, London, 1965, vol. 1, p. 636).

international financing is mandatory to be able to produce at all.

The aviation industry with its supersonic aircraft, space exploration and space telecommunications provide three classic examples of this. In the first case only a Franco-British project, the Concorde, has any hope of staying abreast of similar schemes in Russia and America. In the second and third cases the ELDO and ESRO projects required the combined resources of all the West European capitalist powers, not only those of the Common Market.[2] It seems likely that the production of nuclear energy for peaceful purposes will ultimately be uneconomical on a national basis and that European financing will be necessary for that too.

The progress in nuclear energy shows how new forces of production burst through the bonds of private ownership: without resort to state subsidy and state financing, not a single capitalist country would have been able to provide itself with a nuclear industry based on private capital alone. The same applies to the aviation and space industries. They all conform to the more general formula according to which the development of productive forces not only transcends private ownership but also the limits of the nation state.

2. The ELDO project is to build a European rocket, Europa I. Britain is building the first stage, France the second and West Germany the third. Italy will be responsible for an experimental satellite, Belgium for the control system and Holland for long range measurements. The ESRO project is to put satellites in orbit which will be used for telecommunications. It is financed by the European Space Research Organization which is supported by ten countries and financed as follows (see *The Times*, 8 May 1967): Great Britain 25%, West Germany 22·56%, France 19·14 per cent, Italy 11·17%, Sweden 5·17%, Belgium 4·42%, Holland 4·24%, Switzerland 3·43% and Denmark 2·21%. The tenth participant, whose name does not appear in *The Times*'s list and whose share is 2·26%, is Spain. Both ELDO and ESRO are at present undergoing a crisis (see p. 59 below).

Without government money and without international financing, Europe cannot build supersonic aeroplanes or satellites.

Technological sophistication in Europe is bound to increase the number of cases in which international capital interpenetration is an *absolute* precondition of profitable production. But leaving these aside, our concern now is with those cases where the establishment of industries of sufficient size is not absolutely but relatively dependent on the internationalization of capital.

In theory, West Germany, France and Italy might be able to sink sufficient capital to set up large competitive computer industries in each of these three countries. But this hypothesis is unrealistic for two reasons. First, it goes against the principle of spreading risks – more capital would be sunk in one sector of industry than its expected profits could justify. Second, three similar firms would lead to massive over-production. There are not enough buyers in the European or the world market for three such firms. There is, therefore, a *relative* necessity for the interpenetration of capital: given the size of the market, in an ever-increasing number of branches of industry there are only a limited number of companies which can operate at a profit. The Common Market therefore simply has no room for four or five big companies in these sectors. Servan-Schreiber quotes the example of the latest developments in the electronics industry – integrated circuits. At the moment, the European market can only absorb 250,000 such components. However, experts estimate minimum sales for profitable production are about a million, so that Europe has only scope for one such business and even then it can only envisage making a profit in the 1970s or 1980s.[3]

3. Jean-Jacques Servan-Schreiber, *The American Challenge*, Atheneum, New York, 1969, pp. 166 *et seq.*

Nevertheless, even in those sectors where two or three large companies can still exist side by side, the benefits of collaboration and amalgamation are so evident that it seems impossible to match the size and competitive capacity of the American giants without resorting to mergers.

This is why the trend towards capital interpenetration between nations has begun to become fact. Besides the two examples which were cited in Chapter 3, one in the photographic and one in the iron and steel industry, a host of examples might be given. The merger of Schneider and the Banque d'Indochine (France) with Empain (Belgium) is of particular significance, because it is the first example of a direct merger between two great financial groups from different countries.[4]

As examples of the same trend, instances of increasing cooperation by various West European financial and banking groups should also be noted. Six French merchant banks have established links with other European financial bodies: Rothschilds with the Italian Copfa (which controls Fiat), the Banque d'Indochine with the Belgian Cofinindus (which controls the Banque de Bruxelles), the Banque Worms with the Bank of London and South America and the Bank of Scotland, the Banque de Paris et des Pays Bas with the Anglo-American Corporation (the Oppenheimer

4. Naturally the international interpenetration of capital in Europe is not limited to movements between the countries of the EEC. Meynaud and Sidjanski (*L'Europe des Affaires*, Éditions Payots, Paris, p. 64) mention the establishment of a frozen food company, Findus International, by Nestlé of Switzerland and the Scandinavian Marabou-Freia; the Swiss chemical company CIBA, after absorbing the firm of Lumière (France), took over Ilford, the British photographic materials company, in collaboration with ICI. It seems as though the photographic materials industry is particularly prone to the effects of the international concentration of capital. Besides the Agfa-Gevaert and Ciba-Lumière-Ilford mergers, the Italian company, Ferrania, has been taken over by the American Minnesota Mining and Minerals Corporation.

Group), De Neuflize, Schumberger, Mallet et Cie with the German bank Delbrueck GmbH., and the Union Européenne Industrielle et Financière with Midland Marine.

Then there is the practice of leasing industrial equipment, introduced into Europe by Interliase, a company set up by the Banque de Bruxelles, the Banque d'Indochine, the Banca Commerciale Italiana, the Banco Español de Credito, Hambros, a West German and a Dutch bank. The Eurofinance Trust was set up by the Belgian Société Générale, the Deutsche Bank, the Banca Commerciale Italiana, the Crédit Suisse and a Dutch bank.

The Eurosyndicat founded in 1958 in Paris, which has created a joint investment fund, prepares financial analyses and takes part in direct investment, was set up on the initiative of six major Common Market banks: the Berliner Handelsgesellschaft, the Mediobanca of Milan, the Banque Lambert (Brussels), the Pierson, Heldring en Pierson bank (Amsterdam), the French Crédit Commercial, and the Compagnie Financière (Paris). In 1967 the Société Financière Européenne was established. Its field of activity is the Euro-dollar market and it specializes in the financing of 'European' companies. Its promoters are the Dresdner Bank (West Germany), the Banca Nazionale del Lavoro (Italy), the Algemene Nederlandse Bank (Holland), the Banque Nationale de Paris (France), Barclays Bank (Great Britain) and the Bank of America (USA). The Banque Européenne de Crédit à Moyen Terme (European Bank for Medium Term Credits) was founded in 1968 by the following partners: the Deutsche Bank (West Germany), the Crédit Lyonnais and the Société Générale (France), the Amsterdam-Rotterdam Bank (Holland), the Banca Commerciale Italiana (Italy), the Midland Bank and Samuel Montagu and Co. (Britain).

Certain important insurance companies have concluded cooperation agreements, notably the Groupe de Paris (the major private French company), the Allianz-Münchner (the major German company) and the British Commercial Union. The second largest Belgian bank, the Banque de Bruxelles, has offered seats on its board to several leading European bankers representing Barclays Bank (Britain), the Crédit Lyonnais (France), the Mees and Hope Bank (Holland), and the Union des Banques Suisses (Switzerland). This trend towards closer ties and capital interpenetration between European banks and financial institutions is particularly well exemplified by the participation, agreed in March 1968, of the Deutsche Bank, the Amsterdam-Rotterdam Bank, the Midland Bank, and an Italian bank, in the capital of the Belgian-American Banking Corporation and the Belgian-American Banking and Trust Co., both controlled by the Belgian Société Générale. As a result this bank became the biggest European bank in the USA and its name was changed to the European-American Banking Corporation and the European-American Bank and Trust Company.

No less significant is the growing number of cases of close cooperation between top firms in the same branch of industry in several Common Market and other West European countries. Thus the main French chemical company, Rhône Poulenc, works in close collaboration with the German Bayer company, and another giant of the German chemical industry, Farbwerke Hoechst is working in close association with Roussel UCLAF, the second largest French pharmaceutical company. The Compagnie Française des Pétroles (France) and the German Huels company (now taken over by the Bayer Trust) are building a polyethylene plant together at Le Havre. Recently Bayer, Badische Anilin and Farbwerke Hoechst (the three companies which succeeded IG Farben), the French firms of Kuhlmann and Progil, and the Belgian company, Petrochim, have set up a company – Glycolex – for the export of ethylene and propylene oxide.

The German Wintershall company and the French company Potasse et Engrais Chimiques are building a complex together at Ottmersheim, near Mulhouse in Alsace, where ammonia and chemical fertilizer will be manufactured.

The German Osram company, the Dutch firm of Philips, and two French companies, one of which has subsequently been bought out by the Americans, are to build the very latest kind of electric bulb factory in Belgium. The Dutch synthetic textiles trust AKU and the Belgian chemical company UCB have agreed that the Belgians will transfer the ownership of their synthetic textiles factory in Belgium, Fabelta, to their Dutch partners and that the Dutch will hand over the ownership of their celluloid factory in Holland to the Belgians.

In response to the agreement between Siemens and Bosch who dominate the German refrigerator market, their most important German rival, AEG-Telefunken, has made an agreement with the Italian Zanussi company so as to maintain or even extend its share of the electrical appliance market. It seems possible that the Dutch Philips Trust may make some agreement with the largest Italian manufacturer of household electrical goods, Ignis. The Swiss corporation, Brown Boveri and the German Krupp trust are building a nuclear reactor together. Forges et Ateliers du Creuset and the German Hanomag corporation have taken a majority of the shares of Austro-Fiat together. ACEC (Belgium), the Compagnie Générale d'Électricité of France and the Nederlandse Kabelfabriek of Holland have set up the Codeca company in Belgium.

Dassault, the French aviation constructors, are associated with analogous companies in Holland and Belgium, Fokker and Sabca. They are also building a twin-engined civilian jet aircraft with Fiat which will have 130 seats, as well as a military training aeroplane with the Dornier company of Germany. The Fiat-Citroën tie-up needs no comment.

In the realm of international competition for great civil engineering projects, almost all the contestants are international consortiums. The Italian group Impregilo (which is backed by Fiat, and the Immobiliare building company formerly controlled by the Vatican and other Italian holdings) associated with the French Citra Group, successively won the contracts for the Keban Dam on the Euphrates in Turkey, the Mantaro Dam in Peru and the Tarbela Dam on the Indus in Pakistan. In the first case they were confronted by Anglo-American competition, in the second by an Anglo-German consortium and in the third by a German-Swiss combine.

Such developments are not accidental. Employers' organizations recognize, as do the technocrats of the EEC, the necessity of the international interpenetration of capital and they would all like to see it developing as fast as possible. The coordinating employers' association of the Common Market, UNICE, presented the EEC Commission with a memorandum in April 1965 requesting legislation to facilitate the international merger of businesses within the EEC. The memorandum especially stressed that the central purpose of the Commission should be to promote such expansion. A similar memorandum was presented in the summer of 1966. The International Chamber of Commerce demanded facilities in October 1965 for businesses which wished to form international mergers. The president of the West German Employers' Association, Professor Siegfried Balke, and the vice-president of the French employers federation CNPF (Conseil National du Patronat Français), Ambroise Roux, expressed their interest in the formation of 'European companies' at almost the same time.

The establishment of such companies raises extremely complex questions of commercial and financial law which are far from being resolved.[5] Company law differs in each

5. The French journalist, Paul Fabra, published a series of articles in *Le*

member country of the EEC. In Germany and the Nether-
lands the take-over of home-based companies by companies
based abroad is illegal.[6] The EEC Commission would
dearly like to create a new special statute for European
companies. Others, especially in France, would prefer a
compromise solution: the writing into the commercial law
of each member country of an identical paragraph which
would allow the formation of European companies. Both
are classic examples of how the law, the 'social superstructure', is forced sooner or later to adapt itself to
economic reality (the relations of production, the 'social
infrastructure').[7]

Fundamentally the problem which the question of the
European company raises is the juridical danger of allowing
an international commercial legal system to exist side by
side with a national one. The French government wants to
avoid this by laying down a *quantitative* minimum limit to
the establishment of European companies, whereas the
Germans and the Commission at Brussels want to lay down
qualitative criteria, only allowing the establishment of
European companies in those areas where there is a 'European need' (aviation, etc.).[8] Legislation, however, is not the

Monde (29 July 1965 *et seq.*), in which he wittily analysed the problems confronting those wishing to set up European companies. He published some
fairly pessimistic views in the same paper on 20/21 November 1965 concerning the progress which had been made up till then in the establishment
of European commercial law. The latest English work on this subject is
Edward Wall, *Europe: Unification and Law*, Penguin Books, Harmondsworth, 1969.

6. *Bulletin Économique de la Société Générale de Banque* (Brussels), June 1966.

7. A résumé of a memorandum of the EEC Commission on the formation
of European commercial enterprises was read to a press conference at
Brussels on 3 May 1966 by a member of the Commission, M. von der Groe-
ben and was published in *Le Monde* on the following day.

8. *The Economist*, 14 October 1967; *L'Echo de la Bourse* (Brussels), 29
November 1967; and *AGEFI* (Agence Economique et Financière), 16 and 19
November 1967.

only obstacle to the formation of European companies. There are also a host of problems related to patent law as well as to the tax laws of the six different member states. All these problems interlock with one another and it seems almost hopeless to try to solve each one singly without providing a general solution for them all.

Historically, the Common Market arose as the result of previous capital concentration in Europe. For a long time, the development of the major productive forces had been in danger of suffocation within the narrow borders of the nation state. This was especially so in Germany. After two historic failures at violent expansion to the East, the productive forces of West Germany are now trying to find a way out of the narrow confines of their national borders by peaceful commercial expansion. Confronted by the inherent conflict between the bourgeois mode of production and the bourgeois nation state, the European bourgeoisie is attempting the best partial and provisional solution available to it for the moment, the creation of a large free-trade area.

The EEC, however, has provoked further capital concentration, for as the market has extended, competition has become more intense, leading to a new stage of concentration and centralization of capital. Even without taking into account the competition with America, the bigger market makes for larger production units, greater capital concentration, and more rational location of factories and utilization of transport facilities. So far the Common Market has not shown these tendencies as much as had been expected, partly because of the legislative problems encountered by the merging and formation of European companies, and partly because the continuous trade boom from 1958 to 1964 meant that there was simply no economic compulsion to greater efficiency and rationalization.[9] But

9. In a memorandum on the occasion of the tenth anniversary of the foundation of the EEC, the Banque Lambert of Belgium stated that in its

the sooner this 'long expansionist wave' ebbs, the sooner the rate of profit declines, the more the impact of American competition will be felt, and the quicker the time will come when European capital will have to stop considering where factories should be built merely on political or social grounds and base its decisions entirely on the question of profitability.

The recent recession in West Germany provided two cases which gave striking confirmation of this. The great chemical trusts wanted to make the port of Antwerp the capital of the European chemical industry (Badische Anilin went so far as to consider moving its head offices there) and the Ruhr iron and steel industry (following the trend to site steel works by the sea) threatened to remove themselves to the Dutch coast. In fact both moves were only threatened and there is little likelihood of their taking place in a few years, let alone months; but then a few years will have to pass before there is such a thing as European commercial law. But such examples are general pointers. They indicate an incipient tendency and at the same time show what strong counter-tendencies these developments are bound to provoke.

These counter-tendencies are not just a reflection of the general historical law of the 'retardation' of consciousness – in other words, the obvious fact that the collective consciousness of social classes and nations generally lags behind socio-economic reality, which means today, in concrete terms, that many bourgeois and petty-bourgeois in West Europe still think in the old national concepts even though it no longer accords with their class interests to do

---

opinion the trend towards concentration which they had hoped for was, so far, insufficient.

so.[10] There is also the fact that – from the bourgeois point of view – the temporary consolidation of capitalism in Western Europe over the last fifteen years rests on a delicate balance of a number of economic, political and social factors – a balance which a radical rationalization of major industry in the Community might be enough to upset.

A structural crisis in their economy has already provoked social disturbances in various member nations of the Common Market, especially in those regions where 'traditional' branches of industry predominate, such as the Walloon part of Belgium, the North of France, the old industrial region of the Loire, and to some extent Genoa and Trieste in Italy. There was a general strike in Belgium in 1960 – and a local uprising in Trieste in 1965.[11] An analogous structural crisis is at present brewing in the Ruhr. If this trend persists, the entire social equilibrium of European capitalism might be shaken. It would be mistaken, therefore, to call those sections of the upper bourgeoisie who have socio-political reservations about 'pure' economic rationality, reactionary. In a sense they have a broader and more realistic view of their global and class interests than do the industrialists and financiers who want to impose 'rationalization' at any price.

In the last analysis, however, the choice is not between two alternative employers' tactics, the one subtle and the other energetic. For the class interests of Big Capital, the solution of this objective contradiction is to be found in a consideration of the role of the state.

10. There are of course divergent interests amongst the European bourgeoisie. Small and medium-sized businesses (partly because they fear increasing state intervention) are generally more opposed to the international interpenetration of capital than are large corporations (see Maurice Duverger, *Le Monde*, 29/30 October 1967).

11. The barricades went up in Trieste again in June 1968 for similar reasons.

Chapter 5
The Nation State Today

It has become a platitude to point out that the bourgeoisie has fundamentally revised its attitude to the state. A long time has passed since the era of *laisser-faire, laisser-passer*. The capitalist socio-economic order cannot survive nowadays without increasing and repeated intervention by the state.[1] The goal of state intervention is not only to defuse social crises by producing social reforms or by alleviating the most flagrant misery – in order, needless to say, to protect and strengthen the social *status quo* and the private property of big capital on which it is based;[2] it also aims to guarantee directly the profits of the dominant sectors of the big bourgeoisie. As we have tried to show elsewhere, the

1. 'The primary characteristic of this new phase in our development is the determining role which the state is called upon to play in it. Without state backing businesses cannot undertake international competition' (M. Huvelin, President of the CNPF, in *Le Monde*, 12 November 1968).
2. Whenever conflict arises between the objectives of the welfare state and this strengthening of big private capital, the bourgeois state always ultimately decides in favour of capital. That basic rule can be seen in operation today. Almost all European governments have sacrificed full employment – the alleged basis of the welfare state – so as to restrain wage increases by bringing back into existence a 'reserve army of labour', and to strengthen 'work discipline'.

state increasingly becomes the direct guarantor of the profits of these monopolistic or oligopolistic sectors.[3]

The divided soul of the contemporary capitalist – on the one hand world citizen, on the other hardened nationalist and proponent of a 'Europe of Nations' – corresponds to the quite concrete contradiction between the objective tendencies of economic development, the increasing necessity for the productive forces to adjust to the violent technological changes resulting from international capital interpenetration, and the social relationships as a whole which render the very survival of capitalism increasingly dependent on direct state intervention.

Nowhere does this contradiction appear more vividly, either in its objective roots – not to be confused with the private whims of an old man – or in its insolubility, than in the ideology and methods with which General De Gaulle tackled the problems of European integration and competition between Europe and America.

Incontestably some aspects of Gaullist ideas on Europe stemmed from the particular characteristics and weaknesses of French big capital which needs, to a much greater extent than its German counterpart, customs and tariff barriers to protect it from British, Japanese and American competition. Its approach to the Common Market, in contrast to that of German big capital, was always defensive, not aggressive.

3. See E. Mandel, *Marxist Economic Theory*, Monthly Review, New York, 1968, vol. II, pp. 501–7, for the various ways in which the state guarantees the profits of big capital. Jean-Jacques Servan-Schreiber – that representative ideological spokesman of neo-capitalism – now discovers, in *The American Challenge*, that Europe requires a minimum of federal power 'to protect and promote European industry" (p. 153). British employers, for their part, have campaigned with growing success to persuade the state to finance almost all the expenses of research and development of private firms (see the article in *The Times*, 26 July 1968, by Professor Blackett).

The prospect of enlarging the Common Market to include the whole of Western Europe, let alone an 'Atlantic Free-Trade Area', is excruciating to French big capital, while its German counterpart would understandably not have the least objection to such a proposal.[4] Thus many of General De Gaulle's apparently whimsical theories about the role of the nation state in economic life reveal themselves, in the last analysis, to be barely camouflaged rationalizations of a specific state of affairs; namely, that French capitalism had been unable to overcome the intense social and economic crisis of the post-war period except by creating an important nationalized sector and by introducing what is an extensive degree of economic programming,[5] even taking into account the present declining phase of capitalism.

Besides the specifically French aspects of Gaullism, it had, however, two more general characteristics which also find an echo amongst the bourgeoisie of other states in the Community.

First, it represented an attempt to overcome too passive an attitude towards the US claim to exclusive political and

4. The difference between German and French exports provides a straightforward explanation for this. In 1955 France exported goods to a value of $4·8 billion and Germany $6·1 billion. By 1967 these figures had risen to $11·4 billion for France and $21·7 billion for the Federal Republic. In 1968 the value of German exports was double the French. In 1967 German exports to the USA were three times higher than those of France. The following statistics are even more conclusive: in 1966 the United States exported $11 million worth of machines and transport equipment; the same year, West Germany exported $9·2 billion worth of the same category of commodities, and $9·8 billion worth in 1967 (it should be remembered that the population of Germany is a third of that of the USA). Over the same period similar French exports stood at $3 billion in 1966 and $3·3 billion in 1967.

5. On this subject see, amongst others, Pierre Naville, *La classe ouvrière et le régime gaulliste*, Études et Documentation Internationales, Paris, 1964, and Serge Mallet, *Le gaullisme et la gauche*, Éditions du Seuil, Paris, 1965.

military leadership within the world capitalist alliance, and to establish a 'healthier' balance with their major ally who is, of course, also their major competitor. Ultimately this is a logical attempt to adjust, at a political and military level, to the changes in the relations between the big capitalist powers which had taken place at an economic level during the last fifteen years. The crisis in the Atlantic Alliance is no more than a reflection of the fact that the military and diplomatic dominance of the United States is no longer matched by its economic position. The resistance of all the European powers (including Germany) to the treaty for the non-dissemination of nuclear weapons is a measure of their unwillingness to concede to the USA an *absolute* military superiority no longer related to its now only *relative* economic superiority.

The second characteristic of Gaullist ideology which found an echo among the West European bourgeoisie is a certain distrust of the European technocrats in Brussels. The EEC Commission and its successor do not yet constitute a genuine state.[6] But today's bourgeoisie needs an actual state to protect its everyday interests. Therefore it shows a strong tendency to defend its national sovereignty against the embryonic supranationality of EEC officialdom. Sometimes this looks suspiciously as though each national bourgeoisie is haggling over petty advantages, willing to 'lose' a few hundred million marks or francs in one place only in order to 'win them back' somewhere else. Some-

---

6. Though it was in the process of acquiring one of the characteristics of a state – financial autonomy. The original Mansholt Plan for a common agricultural policy assured it an income of over $2 billion a year after 1 January 1972. This would have made it financially independent of the contributions of the member states. This is precisely why De Gaulle made every effort to destroy this plan, thereby unleashing the great crisis of the EEC in the summer of 1965.

times this also takes the form of a general principle, which the former President of Euratom, Etienne Hirsch, has called the principle of a 'fair return'.[7]

Ultimately, these manifestations reflect the perpetual anxiety of each national bourgeoisie about the instability of the social situation in its own country, and its attempts to do all it can to avoid the accumulation there of new explosive material and the outbreak of a fresh crisis.

So much for the rational core of Gaullism. But so long as it refused to recognize the inevitable intensification of international capital concentration within the EEC and the other European countries as their only effective means of defending European positions against the giant American corporations within the capitalist framework, it was bound to lead to an insoluble contradiction. It is sheer utopianism to hope to compete with the American corporations with exclusively French (or Italian or German) resources. The refusal to 'alienate' ownership of 'national' industries or the refusal to allow national companies to merge with companies in other Common Market countries usually precipitates their eventual capture by American firms.

The story of Machines Bull is a classic example of this. Even if the resources of the whole French electronics industry had been pooled it would not have been possible to set up a competitive computer industry in France alone. The amalgamation of the main Dutch, French, Italian and German firms would, however, have been sufficient. The alternative was not: either this firm stays 'French' or it is

7. See *Le Monde*, 25 November 1966. In short, this means that each country tries to get back what it contributes to joint European undertakings, in the form of orders placed with its own industries or expenditure within its own territory. This principle led to a serious crisis in Euratom, which was what caused its final dissolution in December 1968.

'taken over by foreigners'; but either it amalgamates with its European counterparts or it is taken over by the USA. De Gaulle's aversion to supranationality thus paradoxically became American Capital's best ally in Europe.[8]

We have said that the bourgeoisie now needs the daily intervention of the state in economic and social affairs for the maintenance of private property, now increasingly threatened by internal contradictions. However, the radius of action of the bourgeois state must conform to that of the productive forces and relations of production. As long as the principal means of production in a given country are in the hands of the local bourgeoisie, the state is the instrument best adapted for the defence of capital. But if this situation starts to change, if there is a tendency towards interpenetration of capital ownership in Europe, the nation state ceases to be an effective means of defending this increasingly international capital. From then on a new form of

8. The failure of Gaullist policy in the computer industry had a political and strategic sequel. The consequent strengthening of America's monopoly in giant computers led to Washington's attempt to delay the manufacture of the French hydrogen bomb by temporarily forbidding the export of the largest 'electronic brain', Control Data 6600, to France (*Le Monde*, 20 May 1966). In this sense, Serge Mallet's thesis that De Gaulle represented the relatively autonomous tendencies of French 'state capitalism' fighting against American capitalism for the possession of a growing number of private capital sectors in France ('Socialisme et Technocratie', in *Tribune Socialiste*, no. 352, 14 December 1967) can only lead to the conclusion that 'state capitalism' must lose. In the meantime, a second 'Machines Bull affair' has occurred. The Gaullist regime's insistence on a 'French', as opposed to a 'European', regroupment of the electrical engineering industry resulted in the Jeumont-Schneider works (together with the Belgian ACEC works and the Italian firm of Marelle) being taken over by the American Westinghouse Corporation. In spite of the French government's aversion to the controlling interest of the Belgian finance group Eurpaix in the big Schneider trust, Eurpaix was both responsible for the 'sell out' and kept a foothold in the new combine while setting up an independent French computer industry (the so-called 'Plan Calcul').

state will be needed which conforms more closely to the new socio-economic situation. This is the historic cue for the entry onto the scene of supranational European institutions. This is why French Big Business got rid of De Gaulle in the spring of 1969: his personal conception of Europe had become an obstacle to the obvious interests of capital.

To put it another way: today the institutions of the EEC – the European Commission, first and foremost – only constitute a precisely delimited surrender of sovereignty, guaranteed by treaty and jealously controlled by the nation states. At best, they correspond to a loose *confederation of states*. They are far from constituting a new *federal state*.

However, once the interpenetration of capital within the EEC has gone so far that at least an important section of the means of production and distribution ceases to be the private property of this or that national bourgeoisie, to become the property of capitalists of different nationality, overwhelming pressure will build up in favour of a different kind of state – a state capable of defending this new kind of private property effectively. Once private property becomes extensively internationalized it cannot be effectively defended within the framework of a French, German or Italian state. European Capital demands a European bourgeois state as an adequate protector and guarantor of profit. The increasing interpenetration of capital within the EEC, the increasing number of banks and businesses which cease to belong to this or that national Capital and become the property of capitalists in all the member states, constitute the process that creates the material infrastructure for genuinely supranational *state* organs in the Common Market.

So far this process has hardly begun. Hence, the weakness of the Community's embryonic supranational organs, and the zeal with which national governments not only deny them all new rights but make successful attempts to deprive them of rights already guaranteed them under the Treaty of Rome. Today, in five of the member countries, the vast majority of capital is still in 'national' hands.[9]

The era of national big capital and of the nation state has not yet been superseded in Western Europe. Although the EEC survived the 1965 crisis, it would still be premature to say that its future is finally guaranteed.[10] Its decisive moment has not yet struck. We cannot determine precisely when it will; this is a question to which we return later.

One fact is certain: the growing desire to resist American competition, manifest not only in 'autonomous state capitalism' but also clearly expressed by the great European concerns, the increasing consolidation of the EEC, and the growing force of supranational state organs within it, are all parallel processes. They are only different ways of expressing a single basic economic tendency: the increasing international interpenetration of capital within the EEC. Thus they represent a transitional period for the EEC, from its

9. The one exception is the small state of Luxembourg whose biggest industry, the Arbed and Hadir iron works, is controlled by a Luxemburg financial group and by two foreign groups, the French Schneider group and the Belgian Société Générale. Recently, the controlling interest over Schneider has been bought by the Belgian group Eurpaix, so that it can now be said that Belgian capital has gained control over Luxemburg's industry.

10. Economic reality dictated that the only way to get over the 1965 crisis was through closer integration and not disintegration of the EEC, a fact which the author correctly forecast. French big capital could not permit the disruption of the EEC. It cracked the whip at the first round of the Presidential elections of 1965. De Gaulle realized that it was serious and came to heel. To understand French big capital's attachment to the EEC it is sufficient to know that French exports to the EEC have quadrupled between 1958 and 1966. They have achieved a rate of growth faster than that of all the other member states with the exception of Italy. In 1958 French exports to its partners in the Community represented 22·1% of its total exports. In 1966 this had risen to 42% of total exports.

first phase of simply being a free-trade area to the development of real economic integration. If these tendencies are reversed or blocked, the final result must be the disruption of the EEC with a return to economic nationalism and a protective tariff system. The present transitional period may last a few more years, but ultimately there are only these two ways out under capitalism.

Consequently, it is preposterous to suggest that the protagonists or members of the European supranational institutions are American agents or blind instruments of some American plot. History has amply disproved such accusations. The tough negotiations at the end of the GATT Kennedy Round in Geneva showed to what extent European capitalism acting in consort (limited here to the six member nations of the EEC) was more effectively able to compete with American capitalism, and how the supranational machinery of the EEC helped, in fact was able to direct, these joint operations.[11] The only factors which have weakened this united front have been the divergent interests of national capitalism, and it is just these that will disappear, or at least be diminished, when the international interpenetration of capital creates predominately common interests.

Naturally, conflicts between these two opposing tendencies – the drive towards increasing interpenetration of capital within the EEC and the protection of national

11. Admittedly the supranational institutions have up till now fulfilled a predominantly ideological role, since an adequate infrastructure is still lacking. This may often conceal the actual basic process. But, like all institutions, they tend to safeguard their own existence and continuity, and this is what ultimately leads them to favour international interpenetration of capital within the EEC; that is, an increasing emphasis on the special interests of Western European big capital, which are different from those of American Capital (see the speech of the President of the European Court of Justice, Robert Lacourt, at a conference held in Paris on the 26 October 1967, in *Le Monde*, 29/30 October 1967).

capital – more or less coincides with specific differences of
interest within the various branches of industry and financial groupings in each country. These conflicting interests
are masked behind various political bodies and ideologies,
or confused by appeals to passion or sentiment. The frailest
companies, those whose branch of industry is not expanding, and stagnant family businesses usually prefer to take the
easy way out and to allow themselves to be bought up or
taken over by American companies. The wealthier, more
dynamic European businesses generally have a wider
choice and prefer to take the path of European cooperation
and capital interpenetration.

Ultimately, the alternatives are the following: either a
general tendency towards the interpenetration of European
capital, with a greater chance of successful competition with
America, or the disintegration of the Common Market and
a reversion to narrow economic nationalism, leaving the
door wide open to increasing US domination of the world
capitalist system.[12]

The big European businesses are so aware of these
alternatives that they have themselves appealed to public
opinion and taken the initiative where governments have
made no attempt to support European cooperation and have
not even kept their own official promises. This has been
particularly true of space and telecommunication projects.

The European space research projects ELDO and ESRO
have been suffering a severe crisis which is basically similar
to the one which rocked Euratom – due to the stubborn
insistence of the various participant governments on the

12. That this alternative was not a complete fiction was demonstrated by
European industry when it threatened to respond to an American threat not
to lower 'the American selling price', promised in the Kennedy Round, by
raising the tariffs on American goods coming into Europe. The devaluation of
the pound also demonstrated the danger of slipping back into economic
nationalism.

application of the principle of a 'fair return'. 150 companies in Britain, France, West Germany, Italy, Switzerland, Sweden and Holland, all members of Eurospace, published a manifesto in November 1967 which supported the setting up of a European telecommunications system using artificial satellites. They also asked for the establishment of a European 'space authority', on the model of the American NASA. Moreover, they defined the position quite clearly: this system must be in operation by the end of 1969, otherwise all space telecommunication would risk falling into the hands of the Americans for years to come.[13]

During and despite the Euratom crisis, the Belgo-nucléaire consortium of twenty-eight Belgian companies finalized an agreement with the German Siemens-Inter-atom group and the Dutch Neratoom group to build a fast reactor together. Besides this, Belgonucléaire is working with the British Nuclear Power Group for the joint sale of various nuclear reactors. Under the presidency of Paul-Henri Spaak, it has built up the Inter Nuclear company, in association with the Nuclear Power Group, Snam Progetti of Italy, and Gute Hoffnungshütte (West Germany) for the production and sale of high-temperature gas-cooled Dragon-type reactors.[14] Despite the impasse over Britain's entry into the Common Market, Eurocontrol, the

13. *AGEFI*, 16 November 1967; *The Times*, 13 December 1967. The ESRO crisis has driven four private companies in the space industry into close collaboration – Matra (France), Erno (West Germany), Saab (Sweden), Hawker-Siddeley Dynamics (Britain). Together with the Belgian Belgospace consortium they are making desperate efforts to retain the orders they have already won.

14. *La Libre Belgique*, 23 November 1967; *AGEFI*, 7 December 1967 and 2 October 1968. Another expression of the Euratom crisis is the construction of two nuclear power stations separately by Germany and France in Baden and Alsace instead of one station together in Alsace. The two separate stations will not be economically viable.

European air security group, has decided to construct an automatic data-processing centre in France, to be built jointly by the British Marconi Company, the French Compagnie Internationale pour l'Information, Standard Electric Lorenze of Germany and Sait Electronics of Belgium.

The direction in which the leading concerns are tending is clear. By taking their own international initiatives and by establishing international companies, they are trying to counteract the relapses in European economic integration caused by the indecision of national governments.

Extra stimulus to do this is provided by the fact that when European capital interpenetration is lacking, US concerns stand, paradoxically, to profit more from the Common Market than those of Western Europe.[15] There is no bar in commercial law to the centralization of American subsidiaries in Europe, whether as holding companies in Luxemburg, or as technical coordination centres in Geneva, Lausanne or Brussels. The rapid extension of American banks throughout Europe facilitates such centralization, which allows US concerns to become more effective throughout Europe than their European rivals.[16] The financial potential thus generated even leads to projects which threaten the most important European concerns, like the attempts (since averted) by General Motors to buy up Fiat, or of a US oil company to buy Petrofina, the biggest corporation in Belgium. Finally it is only a sign of the times if General Motors' attempted takeover of Fiat should have led to the eventual merger of Fiat and Citroën, whether De Gaulle liked it or not.

15. It is, in fact, doubly paradoxical because one of the most important reasons behind American businesses establishing subsidiaries in the Common Market area was precisely to avoid EEC external tariffs.

16. *The Times*, 8 May 1967 and 13 December 1967.

Chapter 6
Britain's Entry into the Common Market

All the arguments we have given only highlight the reasons why British Capital is re-examining its traditional positions and seeking membership of the Common Market. It does so with little enthusiasm, for it is a class which less than fifty years ago still believed itself to be the world's leading power and which is now forced to admit that it cannot go it alone. Behind this change lies first and foremost a shift in the pattern of Britain's trade, which clearly shows that the sterling area – the final outcome of the Empire – is now no longer able to guarantee the growth of British exports.

Table 6

Britain's foreign trade (percentages to each area)

	1953	1962	1966
Sterling Area	47	33·9	31·4
Western Europe	27	37·1	37·6
Common Market countries	13·1	19·4	19
North America	12·4	14	16·7
Eastern Europe	2	2·8	2·9
Other countries	11·2	12·2	11·4

The danger that British exports to the Common Market may stagnate or even fall casts a shadow over the whole of Great Britain's industrial future.

However much Britain's volte-face during the Macmillan government may have been precipitated by considerations of immediate commercial interest, there was also a more serious reason for her turn towards the EEC. This was simply that British Capital realized that the appearance of 'European' firms, through the interpenetration of capital in Common Market countries, capable of reaching the size of American corporations, would ultimately no longer leave British industry any room for an independent place in the world market. It would have to be ruthlessly squeezed between these giants. It was thus forced to apply the old American underworld maxim – 'If you can't beat them, join them.'

Table 7

Businesses employing more than a thousand people

	West Germany		Great Britain	
	1954	1961	1954	1961
Industry overall	708	1,045	1,054	1,206
Export industry	571	854	689	814

With the exception of a few firms in the world class, Shell, BP and ICI, most British firms are about the same size as firms in the Six. The reason that there are more firms in Britain whose employees exceed a thousand than in West Germany is above all because capital concentration in firms working mainly for the home market is further advanced there. Study of those branches of industry chiefly concerned with exports shows that, already in 1961, the number of similar firms was larger in Germany than in Britain. Since then this trend has only increased.[1]

The Coal and Steel Community published a report on 10 March 1967 on the biggest industrial enterprises in the EEC and Great Britain based on 1965 turnover. Of the 50 largest European businesses, 11 were British and 21 German; of the 90 largest, 19 were British and 41 German. The position may have changed following swifter capital concentration in Britain than on the continent. According to a recent study in *Fortune*, of the 200 largest European and Japanese firms at the end of 1967, 53 were British, 43 Japanese, 25 German, and 23 French.[2]

In face of American competition, the relatively smaller size of British firms puts them at the same disadvantage as their counterparts in the Common Market and they are just as unable to overcome this handicap on their own. The only rational solution available to them is to participate in the interpenetration of capital within West Europe. However, because of the necessary congruence of the radius of action of economy and state, such participation only makes sense if Britain joins the Common Market. Otherwise British Capital would be compelled to submit to legal, fiscal and

1. *Journal of the National Institute of Economic and Social Research*, no. 38, November 1966.
2. Britain also seems to have the biggest companies in banking, insurance, etc. Of the 200 largest non-American companies in the capitalist world, 28 were British compared with only 19 German and 12 French. Recently, too, there have been an increasing number of mergers between big British companies - e.g. the merger of General Electric first with Associated Electrical Industries then with English Electric, the merger of BMC and Leyland, and the proposed merger between the National Provincial–Westminster and the Barclays–Lloyds–Martins group of banks. This monster bank would be the second largest in the world, with even bigger credit facilities than the largest American bank.

commercial constraints over which it had no political influence.

Perceptive leaders of British Capital are well aware of the situation and have often brought it up during the discussion on British entry to the Common Market. ICI states that it wants to concentrate its efforts on the European Market. *The Times* says simply that for the aviation industry, 'the British domestic market is the European market'.[3] The debate, meanwhile, proceeds at two levels, in Britain itself and amongst the members of the EEC. Those who wish Great Britain to join the Common Market emphasize two aspects of the overall situation: Britain's ability, once she has become a member of the EEC, to maintain her industrial status (i.e. her ability to compensate for the loss of a part of her domestic market to her partners in the Community by improving her position on the continental market), and her ability to reinforce European industry as a whole against American competition.

At the moment Britain's ability to compete inside the Common Market is limited by the high protective tariffs enjoyed by numerous sectors of British industry. Once Britain joins the Market these barriers will fall. However, there are significant branches of British industry whose competitive capacity seems assured by the degree of their

3. *AGEFI*, 12 October 1967, and *The Times*, 13 December 1967. The Wilson government's change of position on the Common Market arises among other things, from Britain's inability to defend the Commonwealth with her own resources, especially in the realm of air defence (see Nora Beloff's article, 'What Happened in Britain after the General said No', in *From Commonwealth to Common Market*, ed. Pierre Uri, Penguin Special, Harmondsworth, 1968, pp. 64–5). In this sense De Gaulle's remarks about Britain's 'special relations' with the United States are only a half-truth. The same objective forces which thrust British Imperialism into the Common Market compel it to integrate its military forces with those of continental European capitalism.

technological advance, productivity or organization. Various British institutions have made detailed analyses of the situation in each sector of industry. Their results do not entirely agree, but generally it seems as if the computer industry, chemicals, the motor industry, the electrical industry, textile machinery, woollens, and the rubber industry will be the greatest beneficiaries of Britain's entry into the Common Market, while shoes, cotton, clothing, metallurgy, machine tools, and probably iron and steel will suffer.[4] Large British multiple stores and food suppliers may also do well; it is likely, however, that the producers of electrical household goods such as television sets and refrigerators will do poorly.

The representatives of British big capital have lost no chance of holding the advantages of Britain's entry to the Common Market before their potential partners. Sir Paul Chambers, then chairman of ICI, Britain's largest company, speaking in Paris on 19 January 1967, fully expressed all the disquiet which America's accumulated superiority on the international market inspired in British industry. He stressed that 75% of all drugs sold in England were either made under American licence or were made by American subsidiaries. He concluded by saying that Britain's entry into the Common Market would help West European technology to close the gap with American technology.[5]

Bourgeois politicians have not been slow to adopt the theses of big business. Harold Wilson has suggested the foundation of a 'European Technological Community'. He was speaking, it is true, of collaboration at government level to finance technological research and development, but this only confirms the fact that those branches of industry which are heavily dependent on research cannot function without state support.[6] However, the formation of great European companies is the only certain way of diminishing the ever-increasing American dominance in this area.[7]

The computer industry is the best example of this. 80% of the computers now in use in the EEC are American. An explosion is now forecast in the electronic computers' market. It is estimated that the number of computers required is going to increase three to four times in the coming years inside the Common Market. After the take-over of Machines Bull by the American General Electric corporation, the French government agreed to a subsidy of $40 million to make the French computer industry competitive by merging four small companies. This is not an ambitious project, however. In Western Europe the only feasible competitor of the American corporations is the British computer industry, and this industry, broken up as it is into a number of medium-sized firms, is hardly a serious rival. Between 1962 and 1967 its share in its own domestic market was reduced from 80%

6. European collaboration in scientific research has produced the strikingly successful European Centre for Nuclear Research (CERN) near Geneva.

7. Wilson first made this proposal in January 1967. In November of the same year he put forward a seven-point plan which contained, amongst other things, an appeal to British employers' associations to intensify their attempts to join European companies. The Bow Group promptly declared that it was in favour of a 'European Common Market of ideas and scholarship' to reduce the brain drain to the USA. In *The Times* (2 October 1969), Christopher Layton wrote: 'In the most advanced industries – computers, electronics, nuclear power – which provide the key to higher living standards in the future, Britain still has important assets. But these most of all need a continental market, public and private, and could lose out badly if Britain is on the fringe of the industrial integration of the next decade.' (The same author recently devoted an essay to this subject in *European Advanced Technology*, P.E.P., London, 1969.)

to 45% by the incursion of computers designed or made in America. So various sources in Britain have concluded that by the 1970s and 1980s only one united European company will be a match for the American challenge.[8] In fact feelers had already been made in the past for Anglo-French (or even British, French, Dutch and German) collaboration in this field, and it is probable that had they been successful Machines Bull would not have been taken over by American capital. De Gaulle's opposition was to a considerable extent responsible for frustrating these negotiations.[9] One should note that the main European producer of semi-conductor components, the Italian firm SGS is also the main European producer in Britain, France and West Germany – through its subsidiaries established in these countries – but is now looking for a link-up with other European companies be-because it is suffering from a shortage of capital.

The short-range Airbus with its high passenger load is another example. At the moment an American company,

---

8. *The Times Business News*, 27 August 1966; *The Economist*, 21 January 1967. In the middle of 1968 the three main British computer manufacturers, International Computers and Tabulators, English Electric Computers, and Plessey, merged.

9. At the end of October 1967 a new small step was taken for the sharing of information between the British Elliot Automation and the French Compagnie Générale d'Automation. Siemens, the largest West German trust, with a payroll of 270,000 of whom 30,000 work abroad, tripled its sale of computers between 1965 and 1967 and will have increased it sixfold by the end of 1968. It already occupies a third of the German market and this share is expanding rapidly. It is admittedly associated with the American electronic corporation RCA (small in comparison with IBM and General Electric) but the major source of capital in the association is German. In association with Philips – which seems about to make a breakthrough in the information industry – and with the new British electronic consortium, it could constitute a serious threat to the large American computer corporations.

Lockheed, has the world monopoly of the construction of this type of aeroplane. Britain, France and West Germany were trying to construct a comparable prototype together, the Airbus A 300, which will carry three hundred passengers. To maintain its monopoly Lockheed tried to win the British away from the project. However, without their participation, the scheme ceases to be either profitable or realistic.[10]

The Economist recently pointed out that besides the Airbus project and the plan to build a particle accelerator for CERN, also not yet ratified, there were no less than eleven European projects with British participation under way: Concorde, the Anglo-French strike aircraft Jaguar, the Anglo-French helicopter WH13, ELDO, ESRO, Eurocontrol (the European military air traffic control system, NADGE, CERN, Comsat (the international space telecommunications system), the Channel Tunnel, and Martel, the Anglo-French rocket. In addition to these projects there is the Anglo-German fighter, Eurojet, which is being built by the British Aircraft Corporation and Messerschmidt-Boelkow, the British, German and Dutch project to enrich uranium by ultra-centrifugation, and the MRCA-75 multiple-purpose jet fighter built jointly by Britain, Italy and West Germany, which gave Rolls-Royce an order worth £600 million – the biggest ever for a European aircraft company. The total value of the British contribution to these eleven projects amounts to some 2·5 billion dollars.[11] In this context it is also worth noting that many British interests threatened to pull out of these communal projects, e.g. Concorde, the Airbus, ELDO and CERN, in

10. *L'Echo de la Bourse* (Brussels), 5 December 1967.
11. *The Economist*, 18 November 1967; *Le Monde*, 6 September 1969.

response to De Gaulle's veto on British entry into the Common Market.[12]

All these projects depend on the public sector. In addition there are numerous Anglo-European projects in the framework of strictly private industry. A few of these, in the fields of banking and finance, have been mentioned. Besides these there is the sensational proposal of the Anglo-Dutch company, Shell, that they and the Italian companies Fiat, Fincantieri, Finsider, Finmare, Lloyd Triestino and Assicurazioni Generali di Trieste should centralize the whole European citrus fruit market in the ports of Genoa and Trieste. The proposal hinges on the construction of a fleet of twenty-five container ships at a cost of $60 million.[13] The collaboration in the electronics industry between Ferranti (UK) and Solvay (Belgium) is a reflection of the same tendency. The Nitrex cartel which the European corporations have set up for the export of chemical fertilizer has made similar proposals to three British firms: ICI, Shellstar and Fisons. ICI has founded a common company with the German firm of Degussa for the production of siliconized filling material. Both firms provide 50% of capital. British Leyland, the main British automobile company, has signed a cooperation agreement with Renault – an obvious move to offset the pressure from the Fiat–Citroën deal.

De Gaulle's opposition to Britain's entry into the Common Market comprised two paradoxical elements. First, by shutting Britain out of the EEC he lost the one ally who might effectively have opposed what he feared most: the

12. *The Economist*, 16 December 1967; *The Times*, 5 July 1968; *Le Monde*, 12 July 1968; *The Times*, 29 July 1968; and *L'Echo de la Bourse* (Brussels), 26 June 1968. The private Society of British Aerospace Companies responded to this threat by a direct appeal to public opinion.
13. *The Economist*, 24 June 1967.

rapid development of supranational powers in Western Europe. Having been formerly so powerful, it is natural that no other nation in Western Europe is so deeply attached as Great Britain to its belief in national sovereignty. Second, a Europe independent of the USA would be considerably more viable and competitive if Britain's economy and technology were at its disposal.

De Gaulle's insistence upon the special ties between the United States and Britain and upon the maritime basis of the British economy were hardly convincing. It showed how little he understood the transitional situation of British imperialism, between the decline of the Empire and its decision to enter the Common Market. For it is precisely its determination to tackle this difficult problem, which proves British Capital's resolution to close one epoch of its international relations and to enter another closer to its own basic interests.

In this respect, an old man's inability to transcend the nationalist beliefs of his youth were undoubtedly at work. De Gaulle's 'great plan' to establish French political hegemony on the continent of Europe by sapping American superiority and exploiting the French monopoly of nuclear weapons could not tolerate the admission of Britain to the Common Market. But this plan was utopian through and through; it sought a position for French capitalism which was not commensurate with its real economic and political strength. This was the true reason why his veto of British entry was ultimately bound to fail, just as his attempts to delay or prevent the growth of the EEC, which are almost forgotten today, also failed. The most he could hope for was long-term obstruction until economic and physiological reality eliminated him. In the end, in May 1969 the French bourgeoisie got rid of De Gaulle for reasons of economic necessity.

Is it conceivable that the British upper class would not only be willing to associate with European companies but would also agree to relinquish national sovereignty so as to allow the emergence of a new supranational state in Europe? Such a question still seems a purely hypothetical one today, for there are still considerable bonds between Britain and the Commonwealth.[14] The value of the goods exported to the Commonwealth still exceeds the value of goods exported to Western Europe by 50%, and these ties still affect the beliefs and emotions of the English bourgeoisie out of all proportion.

There is, however, the beginning of a trend in the opposite direction, which should not be ignored.[15] Between 1958 and 1965 British exports to the Commonwealth increased by 30%, those to EFTA increased by 109% and those to the Common Market by 116%. The imperial preference system, set up in the heyday of the Empire, is slowly being eroded. In India it has virtually disappeared. In Canada and Australia it is under ruthless attack from American and Japanese competition. In many countries in Africa and South-East Asia it is in immediate danger of the next wave of colonial revolution; meanwhile it is undermined by inter-imperialist competition. In 1967 Britain was overtaken as Australia's number one customer by Japan and the EEC

14. See, however, *The Economist*, 16 December 1967, which states categorically that, 'what is certain is . . . that European development will be a sham . . . if it is not supranational'. This seems to be the credo of at least a section of British big capital.

15. Nora Beloff notes on this subject that Wilson's conversion to the Common Market was occasioned by his disillusion with the economic possibilities of the Commonwealth. 'The Commonwealth no longer existed as an economic concept' (see 'What Happened in Britain after the General said No', op. cit., pp. 59 and 86). The sterling area has practically ceased to be a monetary unit since the Basle Agreements of September 1968 (*The Economist*, 7 September 1968).

did more trade with Nigeria than the UK. Britain's declining financial status – the origin of her military retreat East of Suez – has slackened her grip on markets in which she once had a privileged position.[16]

Economic necessity forces British big capital to turn to Europe. Ultimately it will break down all ideological and sentimental resistence, even to the idea of supranational authorities. This is all the more true since Britain, within the framework of an enlarged Community and with the support of her traditional allies in the Benelux countries, and possibly of Scandinavia, could claim a leading continental position. In the long run only a socialist Britain could make any other choice.

The same economic logic could help her overcome the most serious obstacle to entry into the EEC – the special role of sterling as an international reserve currency and the chronic weakness which goes with it. If European capital is to be integrated effectively then a common European monetary system is essential. The question, therefore, is not whether the pound should 'improve' before Britain can join the Common Market, but whether British capitalists will be willing to allow its absorption into a new European currency, better able to become an international reserve currency than a definitively weakened sterling.

16. U. W. Kitzinger, *The Politics and Economics of European Integration*, Praeger, New York, 1964, pp. 191–2, points out that the five stages on the Tories' road to the Common Market were: the Suez affair, the Blue Streak fiasco, Macmillan's failure at the Paris summit, the 1961 rescue operation on the pound by continental banks, and Britain's slower economic growth by comparison with the EEC.

Chapter 7

The Division of the World Market

So far we have only analysed the objective laws of the capitalist mode of production and the interests of the European big bourgeoisie. Obviously, these interests are not the same as those of the working people of Europe, let alone those of the whole of mankind. The history of that mode of production teaches us that, under it, all progress towards the centralization of capital – that is ultimately, any extension of the objective socialization of production – is always full of contradictions. The fact that in a big factory planning is rational only intensifies the competitive anarchy between one big factory and another. In a trust or cartel, rational planning can extend throughout entire sectors of industry, but at the same time it exacerbates the irrationality and anarchy of uneven development and competition between different branches of industry. Under capitalism an 'organized' or 'planned' economy on a national scale means the sharpening of international competition. Regional economic integration only accentuates conflict, competition, and confusion on a global scale.

The establishment of the EEC was not the origin of the prolonged economic boom which European capitalism enjoyed from the Korean War until 1965. On the contrary, it was this prolonged boom that made it easier to establish the EEC. In a period of stagnation or of economic recession the member states would certainly not have been prepared to accept the lowering of tariffs or a renunciation – however minimal – of economic sovereignty. However this boom, and that of the American economy which began when Kennedy came to power, have aggravated the discrepancy between the expansion of the industrial countries and the stagnation of the underdeveloped countries – a discrepancy which is becoming progressively more dangerous. Over the last fifteen years the rich countries have become richer and the poor countries poorer. There is striking statistical evidence of this. The share of the so-called Third World countries in world trade fell from 31·3% in 1950 to 20·8% in 1963, and had come down to 18·5% by 1967. Without the oil trade its share would be down to less than 10%.

There is no need to emphasize what an obstacle the tariffs of the Six are to the typical exports of the Third World (textiles and food). The same applies to the discriminatory measures taken against the exports of certain Latin American and Asian nations in favour of the tropical products of African countries associated with the EEC.

Exports from the Common Market are also affected. In 1958 the developing countries still bought 27% of all EEC exports. This decreased to 15·7% in 1965, of which 4% went to those countries associated with the EEC. In 1967 this figure even fell to 14·7%, of which 3·5% went to associated countries. In other words, if the People's Republic of China is included, two-thirds of humanity buys hardly more than 10% of the products exported by the EEC. Many specialists regard this development with alarm. It is evidence of the increasing trend of industrialized nations to exchange their industrial products amongst themselves, thus denying the international capitalist economy the safety valve of the exports of industrial goods to non-industrialized countries. The root of this trend is a form of international concentration of income and wealth which cannot be analysed here but which corresponds to a fundamental tendency in the evolution of capitalist production.

The report of the United Nations Department for Social and Economic Affairs for 1963 examined in detail the effects of the EEC's protective tariffs on trade between the EEC and the Third World.[1] So far as goods of a purely tropical nature are concerned, Third World countries are most discriminated against in Germany's import of bananas and wood and in the Benelux countries' import of vegetable oil. Coffee from African countries in the franc monetary zone is correspondingly favoured. However, this discrepancy did not seem to have the overall effects expected. Between 1958 and 1967, EEC imports from associate member states grew from $1·5 to $2·3 billion, while the value of imports from other African states grew from $1 to $2·4 billion, and the value of imports from all Asia, minus China, rose from $1·8 to $2·9 billion. Imports of coffee, tea, cocoa and spices quadrupled between 1958 and 1968 and profited countries such as Nigeria, Tanzania, Colombia and Brazil as much as, if not more than, countries which were signatories to the Yaoundé Convention. The former nations' dislike for the EEC therefore turned into a desire for closer relations – which has gone so far as an attempt to form some kind of association of former Commonwealth countries.[2]

1. United Nations Department of Economic and Social Affairs: *World Economic Survey*, 1962, I; *The Developing Countries in World Trade*, United Nations, New York, 1963.
2. *Statistiques Mensuelles de la CEE*, Série Commerce Extérieur, no. 4 and 5, 1968; Dennis Austin, 'Britain, Commonwealth, Africa and the EEC',

Meanwhile, a few figures give some idea of the extent to which trade between Third World countries not associated with the EEC and members of the EEC has suffered. Between 1957 and 1961 French imports of coffee from these countries fell from 34·7 to 28·1%, the cocoa imports of the Benelux countries fell from 69·5 to 64·9%, Italian imports of wood fell from 93·7 to 79·8%, while their imports of vegetable oil fell from 92·9 to 78·3%.[3] Though total German and Italian imports from non-associated African countries trebled between 1958 and 1967, imports from associated countries quadrupled over the same period. These figures should be contrasted with a 50% growth in West German imports alone from India, Pakistan, Indonesia, Malaysia, and other parts of South-East Asia.

The so-called 'common agricultural policy', which above all favours the French bulk grain exporters, causes manifest discrimination against all imports of food into West Germany. This affects not only meat from Argentina, Uruguay and Australia, but wheat from Canada, cheese from Denmark and fish from Scandinavia. The threat the EEC holds over the import of textiles from developing countries is even worse. Not only are there tariff barriers but the amount imported is limited by quota as well. Thus in 1960 the Common Market states only imported 4% of their textiles from underdeveloped countries, whereas EFTA imported 14% and the USA 22%.[4]

The EEC, it is true, has made substantial loans to associ-

---

in *From Commonwealth to Common Market*, ed. Pierre Uri, Penguin Special, Harmondsworth, 1968; U. W. Kitzinger, *The Politics and Economics of European Integration*, Praeger, New York, 1964, pp. 114–15.
3. United Nations Department of Economic and Social Affairs, op. cit., p. 99.
4. The President of the World Bank, George D. Woods, stated in Paris on 24 January 1967, that international tariffs were disadvantageous to the growth of industry in developing countries.

ated African states. Such credits, however, have primarily benefited Common Market industries and machinery exporters (this is chiefly how West Germany has improved its position on the African market), and have not speeded up the industrialization of these countries. American influence, through trade and military aid, is therefore slowly increasing and has led, at least in the case of two important African countries (Morocco and Congo-Kinshasa), to their being transferred from the European into the US sphere of influence.

The results are even easier to distinguish if the influence of the United States and the European capitalist countries is compared globally. There is no doubt that the USA has succeeded in gaining a strong position in many former colonies and semi-colonies of the West European powers. In South Vietnam, Lebanon, Thailand, Turkey, Greece and Indonesia, Washington has taken over from Paris, London and Amsterdam. Now a similar process is occurring in what are conveniently called the 'white dominions' of the Commonwealth. In Latin America the position is still clearer. In 1966 the United States exported $4·7 billion there, while exports from capitalist Europe were only worth $2·9 billion. In 1938 the value of American exports to Latin America was only $350 million compared to nearly $500 million from capitalist Europe.

This process has certainly not been entirely beneficial to the American economy. It has been partially conditioned by huge military expenditures (the war in Vietnam, for example) as well as by the increase in tension which this war has provoked in American society. But by isolating and contributing to the erosion of some of the key positions of European – particularly British – big capital (for instance European oil interests in Arab countries and the British position in Malaya) there can be no doubt that this process of substitution is shifting the balance of power in favour of America. De Gaulle's clever manoeuvring with the forces of colonial revolution in an attempt to win back political capital for West Europe had little chance of success. First, because his manoeuvres demanded a solid economic base which he lacked, second, because they had already been overtaken by a radicalized revolutionary attitude in the colonial and ex-colonial nations.

The remarkable rise of Japan to the place of third largest power in the world has also contributed to this process. On the one hand, the Japanese assault on world markets, based on its young, highly developed technology, threatens European trade more than American markets. The most strikingly successful Japanese exports are: shipbuilding, transistor radios and television sets, optical goods, and scientific equipment (for instance, electro-microscopes). In the iron and steel industry, too, European and not US companies are the main rivals of the Japanese. The next great surge of Japanese exports will be into the automobile industry. Already she has taken over third place from Britain, and will probably permanently replace West Germany in second place before the end of the 1960s. Her export offensive carries two threats for the European motor industry – to their domestic market and to their share of the American market.

On the other hand, American corporations have secured a very strong position in the Japanese market, to which European firms have no equivalent. At the moment Japan is beginning to liberalize the conditions under which foreign capital can be imported. Certainly the Americans will take the opportunity to inject a massive quantity of their capital into Japan. In fact it is probably safe to predict an increasing rate of American capital export to Japan over the next ten years.[5]

Japanese big capital in its turn is achieving more and more success in winning back, through peaceful commercial expansion and 'development aid', positions in those territories which it lost in 1945 or coveted during the Second World War: the Philippines, Thailand, South Korea, Formosa, Malaysia, Indonesia and even Australia. Japan is even forcing the USA to retreat commercially from these countries to an ever-increasing extent (the sales of American cars in this area have almost melted away before the tide of Japanese exports). In South Korea, Thailand, Hong Kong, Singapore, Indonesia, Malaysia, Burma and Ceylon, the total of Japanese exports is greater than America's. In Formosa and in the Philippines they are running neck and neck but the Japanese share is growing faster than the American.

However, while American export outlets are directly threatened by Japan in East Asia, it seems that America will profit from Japanese expansion in the long run, because Japanese firms active in this area depend on the USA for tools and raw materials. Growth of Japanese exports automatically leads to an increase in American exports to Japan, The EEC has no equivalent of this as yet.

The value of Japanese exports to Oceania and Asia grew from $1·138 billion in 1958 to $4·03 billion in 1967. Over the same period the value of Japanese imports from Canada and the USA rose from $1·36 to $3·9 billion. The fact

5. The first year of the liberalization of the import of capital into Japan did not bring the results anticipated by Wall Street. The Japanese remain cautious. But one 'big deal' has already occurred in favour of US penetration: the agreement between Chrysler and the automobile department of Mitsubishi Heavy Industries.

that in 1967 Japan imported five times more goods from the USA than she did from the EEC countries shows how Japan has become a privileged market for American capital. (The difference is of the order of $3·2 billion against $655 million.)

It would be wrong, however, to consider Japanese imperialism simply as a satellite of American imperialism. The pattern of European-American relations at the beginning of the 1950s is repeating itself in Japanese-American relations. After a spell during which the Japanese copied and imitated foreign goods, they are now set to develop their own technological innovations.[6]

In the field of computers, Japan seems to be the only country – besides Great Britain – able to stay in the race behind the United States. Thanks to more and more independent research and the global scale of companies, the drive of Japanese expansion will enable Japanese capitalism to challenge both the United States and Western Europe.[7]

Just as American trade with Japan far exceeds that of Western Europe, the latter's trade with the Eastern bloc far

6. There are some interesting details on this subject in the *Far Eastern Economic Review*, no. 32, 8 August 1968. The Japanese have made breakthroughs in lasers, nuclear medicine, electronics and advanced automobile design. The total value of Japanese expenditure on research and development rose from $1 billion in 1964 to $1·7 in 1968 and will probably reach $3·5 billion in 1970.

7. The merger between Yawata Steel and Fuji Steel created the world's second largest steel company, producing 21 million tons a year, far more than any of its European rivals. The largest Japanese bank has more deposits than the largest German bank. To date three combines between world giants have taken place in Japan: Shell and Mitsubishi have set up the petrochemical complex at Yokkaichi near Nagoya. Péchiney and Mitsui are building an aluminium plant in Kyushu, and Texas Instruments are making integrated circuits with Sony. Ford has recently concluded an agreement for a joint venture with Nissan Motor and Toyo Kogyo to produce automatic gearboxes in Japan, to be owned 50% by Ford and 50% by the Japanese corporation.

exceeds that of America. Official US government discrimination against trade with the Eastern bloc, especially
the trade in so-called strategic materials, and the general
fear that modernization of Russian industry will lead to
greater Soviet military potential, have forced the US bourgeoisie to display the greatest caution in trading with the
Soviet Union and Eastern Europe. Over the last few years,
it is true, American trade policy with the East has been
modified. After conditions for credit and trade with Yugo-
slavia had loosened, the export of American goods to
Poland and Rumania became easier. Nevertheless, the
expansion of American trade with countries of the Eastern
bloc has remained far smaller than that between those
countries and West Europe. The same applies to trade with
the People's Republic of China, virtually non-existent for
the USA, while capitalist Europe has enthusiastically
exploited the opportunities presented by the Soviet blockade of China.[8]

The great American trusts have vainly attempted to
prevent this development, which is much to their disadvantage. They have exerted continual pressure, through
Washington, on their European allies to prevent the export
of so-called strategic materials to the East, and at the same
time they have tried to persuade the American government
to relax its restrictions on American exports. So far the
results have been nugatory.

Between 1958 and 1967 the value of exports from the
EEC to countries of the Eastern bloc rose from $624
million to $2·1 billion. Over the same period the value of

8. In 1967 the gross value of trade between the People's Republic of
China and non-capitalist countries was only $865 million, while the value
of trade between China and capitalist countries was $3·2 billion, Japan had
the lion's share of $621 million, Canada exported $170 million worth of
wheat to China and EEC exports were worth $408 million, half from West
Germany, half from France.

American exports only rose from $110 to $198 million. Just as Japan represents a privileged market for America, so the Eastern bloc represents a privileged market for Western Europe.[9] The sale of computers provides a striking illustration of this. In the next few years the Soviet Union is going to automate its industry and aims to integrate mathematical methods into economic planning (operational research and linear programming). There are therefore an ever-increasing number of uses for computers there. Up till now this is the only part of the world where the market has been dominated by the British electronics industry.[10] Specialists regard the Soviet Union as lagging five years behind the West and as needing 12,000 computers with a total value of $10 billion. Although Japanese competition for this market was expected it has not yet made itself felt.[11]

Since mid-1966 the Eastern bloc has not only been a privileged market for Western Europe. A stage has been reached where it is possible to make modest exports of capital from the imperialist West to the East. The building of industrial complexes has been matched by long-term credits with interest rates such that they can be described as capital investment. The most important examples of this are: the construction of a colossal automobile plant worth $875 million at Togliattigrad (USSR) by Fiat, the construction of an automobile plant in Rumania, the construction by the Pirelli company of six synthetic rubber factories in the USSR, ICI initiatives in establishing numerous petrochemical complexes, and a Dutch company's construc-

9. The total value of exports from Western Europe (the Six plus the Seven) to Eastern bloc countries in 1967 rose to $3·2 billion. West Germany had the largest share – 26% – with Great Britain second (16%).
10. *The Economist*, 24 December 1966 and 19 August 1967.
11. There is an interesting article in *Le Monde* (22/23 October 1967), devoted to the question of whether the USSR had missed the computer revolution.

tion of a market-garden complex in Bulgaria. There are now 150 factories in Eastern bloc countries built by West German firms, some under licence and others on a profit-sharing basis. American companies, however, do receive sub-contracts from some of these investment projects – for instance, some $20 million worth on the Fiat Togliattigrad deal.

From all this it is reasonable to conclude that the world market does not fundamentally alter the power relations between American and West European imperialism. The latter enjoys appreciable trading advantages in China, Africa, the USSR and Eastern Europe, while America has turned Latin America and South-East Asia into its private hunting grounds, while simultaneously increasing its share of the markets of certain countries in the sterling area. The advantages of each side seem to be approximately equivalent. Consequently it is in Western Europe and in North America that the decisive competition between the great monopolies and the imperialist powers is taking place.

At this point it is too often forgotten that the most important sector of the world market is the internal market of the United States itself. The value of imports to the USA rose from $12·7 billion in 1956 to $34·7 billion in 1968. Compared with US national revenue, this is a pittance, a mere 10% of total internal retail trade, which is the very reason why it is susceptible of rapid expansion.

If the interpenetration of capital continues in Western Europe and capital concentration continues in Japan, and if industrial colossi arise in these areas with a production capacity comparable to that of the American giants, they will be poised for successful conquests in the American domestic market. For, with equal technology and productivity, they have a trump card to play: labour costs two to four times lower than those in the United States.

For the moment American trusts still enjoy the economies of size and the advantages of considerable technological superiority which generally allow them to offset their higher labour costs with greater productivity.[12] But once these privileges disappear, the threat can quickly become a reality. Thus the failure of the American iron and steel industry to modernize in the 1950s and early 1960s has already made Japanese and European steel competitive on the US home market, and the import of ferrous goods to the USA has become substantial and accounts for almost 20% of domestic consumption. In the motor industry, imported vehicles exceeded the one million mark for the first time in 1968. In certain industrial sectors – sewing-machines and typewriters – more than 50% of all goods sold in America since 1960 came from abroad. This foreign breakthrough is due to the technological lead which the Italians, Germans and Japanese have established in these fields. A similar state of affairs obtains in shipbuilding where Japan and Sweden are far ahead of the United States.[13]

The fact that this danger loomed up in some sectors of industry was enough to provoke an intense protectionist counter-offensive. At the annual meeting of the International Iron and Steel Institute held in Los Angeles in October 1968 considerable pressure was brought to bear on Japanese and European iron and steel exporters to impose

12. Since 1962 American industry has been undergoing a hectic period of re-tooling and re-equipping, which is, to a large extent, the explanation of the 1962–68 boom. In America between 1960 and 1966 machine-tool production more than doubled, whereas in Western Europe it only increased by 60% and in Japan by 70%. Simultaneously the USA acquired a further technological lead by the rapid production of automated machine tools (controlled by punched tape). In this sector of industry the total value of American output reached $247 million in 1966. Parallel figures for Western Europe and Japan are $34·5 million and $2·7 million respectively.
13. Seymour Melman, *Our Depleted Society*, Holt, Rinehart and Winston, New York, 1965, pp. 48, 56–7, 60–1.

voluntary quota on the tonnage they export to the United States.[14] The Nixon administration has reinforced this tendency, especially towards Japan, whose textile industry is accused of 'flooding' the American market. However, in the long run, American imperialism stands to lose by protectionism more than it can gain. (To put it more precisely: the branches of industry which would lose by European and Japanese reprisals carry greater weight with American big business than those threatened by foreign imports.) This protectionism is itself now being directed against foreign capital investments in the USA, as indicated by the Nixon administration's opposition to the merger between British Petroleum and Standard Oil of Ohio, which was designed to exploit the Alaskan oil finds.

Providing that a wave of protectionism does not entirely alter the present course of world capitalism, the relative success of European capital interpenetration could become a key factor in undermining the social equilibrium of America. An attack by European and Japanese big business on the American home market must unleash the classic capitalist response – an attempt to cut back the growth in real wages and to impose an incomes policy, in other words, reducing wages and union rights. This could profoundly alter the attitude of the US white working class to the system. The sudden end to the rise in real wages for the American workers since the mid-sixties, due mainly to inflation and increased taxation, has already caused a significant increase in trade-union militancy. Annual man hours lost through strikes in the USA rose from an average of 19 million between 1960 and 1965 to 25·5 million in 1966, 42 million in 1967, and 42·4 million in 1968.

14. *The Economist*, 2 November 1968; the *Far Eastern Economic Review*, 30 June 1968; *The Times*, 20 November 1968.

Chapter 8

The International Monetary Crisis

For many years the French government tried to use the chronic deficit in the American balance of payments to reduce America's control of the world's economy and, above all, the power of her corporations in the European market.[1]

This chronic deficit is not the consequence of a deficit in trade; on the contrary, for the last six years there has always been a trading surplus which has fluctuated between four and seven billion dollars a year, though it fell steeply to one million in 1968. The real reasons for the balance of payments deficit should be sought in the export of private capital as a secondary cause and, to an even more decisive

1. Are American capital exports cause or effect of the country's balance of payments deficit – in other words, of American inflation? To put the question in these terms, as apologists of the Gaullist regime did, is to condemn oneself to misunderstand the mechanisms governing the international movement of capital in the era of multi-national corporations. In fact, if American inflation ceased and the balance of payments deficit disappeared, the export of capital would probably be stimulated. Great Britain had a balance of payments surplus for a whole century – from the battle of Waterloo to the pistol shot at Sarajevo – and this did not prevent her from investing £4 billion in gold abroad (Michael Barratt Brown, *After Imperialism*, Hillary House, New York, 1963, p. 75). It was precisely this balance of payments surplus that allowed British capital to finance those investments without inflation.

extent, in overseas military expenditure and 'aid' to foreign governments.[2]

French economic theorists of Professor Jacques Rueff's school believe that the chronic deficit in the American balance of payments is nothing but an expression of the 'permanent inflation' of the American economy. As long as the international monetary system is based on the gold exchange standard, they consider that the USA is able to afford to buy up foreign companies by means of the excess purchasing power which it has itself created at home. Export of these inflationary dollars furthermore stimulates inflation on a world scale. It increases the dollar reserves of the central banks who both issue additional national paper currency on the basis of these dollar holdings, and promptly return the dollars to New York where they earn short-term interest, thus augmenting the amount of money and credit both in these countries and in America. This inflationary vicious circle, together with the risk of a sudden withdrawal of capital invested on short term abroad, threatens to throw us back into an economic crisis like that of 1929–33, so they maintain. Rueff's school and the Gaullist regime influenced by it, saw only one remedy: a return to the gold standard, which would automatically re-establish the American balance of payments, but would also compel American big

2. It should be noted here that the net export of American capital, worth about five billion dollars in 1968, should be offset against a net import of interest and dividends from capital invested abroad. In the same year these totalled 4·8 billion dollars. Like British big capital when it had the Midas touch before the First World War, American Capital can allow itself the luxury of financing capital exports with the interest from capital already invested abroad. If capital exports to Europe stopped, American Capital would have to take more profit out of Europe than it is investing there: exploitation would be intensified.

capital to give up some of the positions it has occupied in Western Europe.[3]

Without doubt, it is in the field of currency reserves that one comes closest to finding a reflection of the loss of the absolute superiority the USA held at the end of the Second World War. In 1938 the USA already had 60% of the world's gold reserves. At the end of the Second World War that proportion had risen to 75%. In 1950 it had fallen to 50%. In that year the USA had a reserve of $22·8 billion, the EEC countries only $3 billion, and Great Britain $3·7 billion. By 1958 the American reserves had fallen to $20·6 billion, while the reserves of the EEC had risen to $11·9 billion. By 1967 the situation had been completely reversed. American reserves were only $14·3 billion while those of the EEC countries had climbed to $24·4 billion. By September 1968 American reserves had risen a little to $14·6 billion and those of the EEC, due to French losses, had fallen slightly to $23·5 billion. To this should be added the fact that between 1950 and 1958 US reserves consisted of gold alone and that today they are only 70% gold. The position in the EEC countries has reversed. The share of gold in their reserves rose from 57% in 1958 to 75% at the end of 1968.[4] As for monetary gold, Europe held $15 billion worth in December 1968 against the USA's $10·5 billion.

3. See, amongst others, Jacques Rueff, *L'âge de l'inflation*, Éditions Payot, Paris, 1963.
4. This partly corresponds to a concerted French attack on the dollar. At the end of March 1967 gold comprised 91·85% of the gross reserves of the Banque de France against an average of 78·11% for the EEC central banks and 71·43% for the Banque de France in 1958. But between 1958 and 1967 the proportion of gold in the foreign exchange reserves of the Bundesbank also rose, from 46·04% to 64%, and similar statistics for the Italian central bank are 50·77 to 68%. The whole responsibility cannot therefore be laid at the door of French policy. Furthermore the inevitable result of a reduction of American exchange reserves was an increased risk of a dollar devaluation.

The Gaullist government's repeated attacks on dollar inflation and its flat refusal partially to support the cost of this inflation by extending the channels of international liquidity created the mounting tension in the International Monetary Fund, where Britain and America were calling for broader means of international payment. For many years it has been plain that international monetary reserves have increased much more slowly than international trade. According to those in favour of a return to the gold standard, the slow rate of increase in gold production – the consequence of a gold price set too low – is the cause of the trouble.[5] The British and Americans retort that the trouble is due to an excessively narrow dependence on gold and to a lack of alternative methods of international payment. The reserves of all the central banks, together with the reserves of the International Monetary Fund, were equivalent to 56% of the value of world imports in 1956. By 1967 that figure had fallen to 33%. Even if the United States is excluded on the grounds that it is a special case, there is still a drop from 41% to 30%.[6]

The West European central banks were forced to defend themselves against this risk by keeping a larger proportion of their total reserves in gold. The increasing danger of a dollar devaluation accentuated the trend towards gold hoarding with the result that in 1966 for the first time none of the gold mined (worth $1·44 billion) found its way into the vaults of the central banks, and their overall stock of gold actually fell by 95 million dollars. The decrease in global central bank gold reserves continued in 1967 and 1968. Rueff's campaign to raise the price of gold obviously encouraged this private hoarding of gold.

5. R. S. Cooke, President of the South African Chamber of Mines, which provides 74% of the gold produced in the capitalist world, stated on 28 June 1967 that the production of South African gold mines could slump to a sixth of its present tonnage in a few years since production costs were continuously rising and gold prices were not.

6. These figures should be contrasted with those of 1938 when gold stocks in the central banks were of greater value than the world's annual imports,

France, recently supported by the other members of the EEC, has argued that it would not be enough to create alternative means of international liquidity so long as the chronic deficit in the American (and British) balance of payments was not made good, for this would only entail the risk of perpetuating and promoting the inflation of the dollar and the pound.

When the partisans of a return to the gold standard are shown the dangerous shortage of international means of payment, they usually retort that revaluation of gold by 50 or 100% would solve the problem for many decades to come. It is futile to point out to them that such revaluation would principally benefit Western Europe which has more gold than the USA ($10-15 billion worth at the end of 1968) and that it also entirely ignores the liquidity problems of underdeveloped countries.

Increasing tension within the World Monetary Fund has increased the danger of a return to monetary anarchy which would certainly foment a return to monetary nationalism. Antagonized by the pinpricks and the barely disguised attacks of French Capital, American big capital has threatened severe retaliation. If the wave of speculation against the dollar were to continue or increase the USA could engage in a series of measures. First, it could contract

---

and with those of 1928 when central bank reserves were worth almost half the value of world imports. International liquidity is in such short supply today that global foreign exchange reserves do not even cover the value of four months' imports, and gold alone covers only ten weeks' worth of imports. As the Gaullist government was sharply reminded in November 1968, the world-wide liquidity crisis is an important factor in exaggerating sudden imbalances and in amplifying the effect of speculative movements. France lost nearly $5 billion worth of gold and currency reserves in less than a year, making the August 1969 devaluation of the franc inevitable. But these losses should be compared with the $10 billion worth of gold owned by the USA for an appreciation of how vulnerable the dollar now is.

the dollar out of its gold warranty (which in fact was done in March 1968); second, it could put an embargo on all gold shipments from the USA (this also became a fact from the middle of 1968 on, when practically all the important central banks of the imperialist countries stopped exchanging dollars for gold); and finally, it could demonetize gold by flooding the market with all its own stock. According to Henry Huess of the American Senatorial committee on financial affairs this would bring the price of gold tumbling down from $35 an ounce to $6.[7] In present circumstances this would very quickly lead to a dollar shortage in the rest of the world. Such a shortage, after being the chief cause of the difficulties of world capitalism in the first years after the war, was thereafter corrected by a US balance of payments deficit. These threats of retaliation have not remained without results: all the imperialist nations, including France, have accepted the creation of so-called special drawing rights ('paper gold') to ease the pressure on the dollar.

7. *L'Echo de la Bourse* (Brussels), 15 November 1967. It is very difficult to calculate the true world demand for non-monetary gold if the dollar were turned into a pure paper currency. The demand for commercial and ornamental gold is estimated to be some half a million dollars a year, about a third of the annual gold production. Debts and bonds in dollars outside the USA are worth about $30 billion of which only a half is privately owned. The value of gold hoarded by individuals in the whole world is estimated to be $20 billion. In recent years it has been rising at the rate of $1 billion a year, a trend which had accelerated since 1965 – confirmed by the $3·2 billion decrease in the gold stored in the vaults of the central banks. Hoarding has absorbed three years' gold production plus $3·2 billion worth, a total of about $7·5 billion worth of gold. Of this, a sizeable share has been bought back by American capitalists through foreign intermediaries since private gold buying is illegal in the USA. After the March 1968 introduction of the 'two tier' gold price – one for the Central banks, another for the free market – most of the current gold production was withheld altogether from the world monetary system. Only in October 1969 did the American monetary authorities agree to South African resumption of gold sales to the Western Central banks.

The Americans believe that the stability of the dollar is not based on their gold reserves but on the colossal productive capacity of the American economy, and the huge volume of commodities thrown annually on the market at home and abroad. The response to such a line of argument and the answer to a unilateral American embargo on gold shipments would be controls on the import of American capital and goods into Europe. This could only produce a return to intense American protectionism whose disastrous results would be the rapid shrinking of international trade and a general depression.

The hypothesis of a full and complete return to the gold standard only strengthens these conclusions. Between 1929 and 1933 the capitalist economy gave a tragic demonstration of how an unfavourable economic situation coupled with a negative balance of payments compels governments who remain on the gold standard to deflate, to restrain credit and overall demand, instead of pursuing a policy of monetary expansion to stimulate economic recovery. The upshot is inexorable; instead of a mild recession there is a severe economic crisis. Those members of Rueff's school who wish to return to the self-regulating mechanism of gold, want, in fact, to roll history back to the era before Keynes.

This is not the place to expose all the fallacies of 'the return to the gold standard' argument. We want to mention only some of the most glaring contradictions.

Rueff and his supporters state that, in an economy based on the gold standard, any loss of gold leads to a decrease in effective demand, leading to a fall in prices which automatically stimulates exports, corrects the balance of payments, and raises the level of employment. They forget, first, that when demand falls off in the domestic market, the utilization ratio of productive capacity starts to fall as well, which in monopoly capitalist conditions often provokes not a decrease but an increase in prices, including the prices of key export goods, since big business is keen to maintain its level of profitability (Wilson's deflation in 1966/67 provides a typical example). Second, they leave out the fact that price is not the only criterion of exportability, that there are fluctuations in the demand for export products and in the nature and variety of exports. Third, they forget that fluctuations in foreign demand also affect export possibilities. So when many countries simultaneously experience a decline in employment levels and effective demand no deflationary measure, no matter how severe, can stimulate exports. The partisans of the gold standard talk as though only monetary crises occur and never crises of over-production. They overlook the fact that between 1815 and 1914, despite the gold standard general to the West, there were many economic crises some of which were very severe.[8]

No one would deny that for many years the United States has been undergoing a typical state of permanent inflation, but it is also true that the huge American industrial machine can only sell a sufficient amount of its output thanks to the enormous debts of the state, companies, and private citizens[9] which are continuously growing. Any attempt to return to financial orthodoxy would lead at a minimum to stagnation and possibly to a chain of recessions. If we were to return to the gold standard these recessions would cer-

8. In *La monnaie et les systèmes monétaires*, by Bertrand Nogaro, published as long ago as 1948 (Eng. tr. *A Short Treatise on Money and Monetary Problems*, Staples Press, London, 1949), there is a vigorous refutation of the dogma of the gold standard. See also Robert Mossé, *Les problèmes monétaires internationaux*, Éditions Payot, Paris, 1967.

9. Net private indebtedness in the United States increased from $140 billion in 1945 to $753 billion in 1963. In 1945 it was equivalent to 78% of gross private income and in 1963 to 143% (Harry Magdoff, 'Problems of United States Capitalism" in *The Socialist Register*, Monthly Review, New York, 1965, p. 68). By 1966 the sum had reached the figure of $965 billion and gross private indebtedness had passed the $1,000 billion mark.

tainly lead to a severe economic slump.[10] In the present situation, American big capital must avoid such an outcome at all costs, for obvious political, social, and military reasons. Consequently a return to the gold standard, dear though it may have been to the Gaullist regime, is pure fantasy.

It is worth recollecting that gold is a commodity whose value is also determined in the last analysis by the amount of socially necessary labour which produces it, and not by 'the demand of international liquidity'.[11] A general return to the gold standard could not itself determine any fixed 'price' for gold. The value of gold would determine the price of commodities. It is quite possible that if it were worked out in terms of hours of labour, the value of gold would be much higher by comparison with the average value of goods today than in, say, 1913, 1929 or 1938. Probably the productivity of gold-mining has not risen as fast as the productivity of other branches of industry; but all that means is that the gold-equivalent values of certain goods have fallen considerably. (What a disaster for capitalism!)

10. The attempt at orthodox budgeting led to quasi-stagnation of production and incomes in the Eisenhower period. In fixed prices, per capita consumer spending rose from $1,723 per annum in 1955 to $1,847 in 1961, a rise of 1·2% a year. There was a recession in 1957/58 and another in 1960/61, in other words the inter-cycle period shrank to three years. In the first nine months of the 1957/58 recession, industrial production fell 13·1% (compared with 15·9% in the first nine months of the 1929 world economic crisis). The United States was only saved from a second 1929 disaster by an inflationary monetary policy and by immense public, especially military, expenditure (see *Economic Report of the President, together with the Annual Report of the Council of Economic Affairs*, U.S. Government Printing Office, Washington, January 1962; and Geoffrey Moore, 'Measuring Recession', in *The Journal of the American Statistical Society*, June 1958).

11. Victor Perlo, who calls himself a Marxist, sometimes seems to forget this (see 'La crise du système monétaire capitaliste' in *La Nouvelle Revue Internationale*, nos. 10–11, 1968).

Even theorists like Rueff who are in favour of a return to the gold standard would not like to establish the value of money exclusively on the value of gold. The copious issue of paper money glosses over this decrease in the value of gold which capitalism could hardly otherwise survive. The inherently stupid phrase, 'the price of gold' – which Rueff would like to see doubled – is both a camouflage for and expression of the permanent inflation to which the system is condemned.[12]

There can be no doubt that ultimately the extension of public and private indebtedness in the United States, accompanied by a permanent drop in the purchasing power of the dollar, can only lead to considerable economic disorder which is bound to affect the international monetary and commercial system. Modern capitalism is beset by the inherent and objective contradiction between the dollar's role in upholding the level of economic activity inside the USA and its role as the principal instrument of international payments. But as it would not be very rational to precipitate a crisis in the next two or three years to avoid a storm due in fifteen years' time, the American upper bourgeoisie will make no attempt to resolve this contradiction by abandoning its anti-crisis monetary policy (i.e. inflation). The Gaullist solution was equally irrational in so far as an acute American economic crisis would have disas-

---

12. As price is the monetary expression of value, and gold is the standard of prices, 'the price of gold' can only be expressed in gold and is therefore a meaningless expression. The formula 'an ounce of gold is worth 35 dollars' does not express the price of gold, but the official value of a paper currency, the dollar. 'Doubling the price of gold' really means halving the official value of a paper currency – after its buying power has already more than halved since 1934. This process, however, tells us nothing about the relation between the value of an ounce of gold and that of a hundredweight of wheat or a ton of steel over the last thirty-five years, the only relation which could tell us, in hours of labour, whether gold is 'over-' or 'under'-valued at different equivalent rates in dollars.

trous consequences on the European capitalist economy. This is further evidence of how wrong it would be to assume that because the American economy has lost its *absolute* superiority it has also lost its *relative* dominance. The American economy is, and will remain for a long time, the most important component of the international capitalist system; to shake it means to shake the whole system. In so far as it was not pure blackmail, Gaullist policy was only an objective indication that certain sectors of the French upper bourgeoisie wanted to saw off the branch on which they were sitting.[13]

We already have one example which shows the consequences of bringing too much pressure to bear on the American economy to reduce the deficit in its balance of payments, and it hardly speaks in favour of the Gaullist thesis. One of the significant components of the deficit in the balance of payments is, as has already been said, the export of capital by the great American monopolies. At present the American government is counselling these corporations to exercise restraint; but to invest all their accumulated capital profitably, they are compelled to invest part of it in Europe. The ideal solution of this difficulty for American companies is to raise the capital to cover their needs on the European market. In other words, European banks lend American companies the capital which enables them either to deprive European firms of some of their outlets or even simply to buy them up. The European bankers do not do this because they are pro-American but only because American big business can offer them better

13. The events of May 1968 and the financial crisis of November of that year demonstrated the extreme vulnerability of France's capitalist economy. In four days France lost a quarter of her reserves and on two occasions the franc was only saved by the massive support of the central banks (especially that of the USA). A year later devaluation inevitably occurred.

securities, higher rates of interest, and wider profit margins.[14]

In the 1966 report of the International Monetary Fund the total value of money invested by American subsidiaries in Europe between 1962 and 1966 was estimated to be $22·5 billion, only a quarter of which – $5·8 billion – came directly from the USA. The figures show that the role of dollars (that 'depreciated paper currency') in buying up 'our businesses' has been grossly exaggerated. The international inflationary influence of the dollar and pound holdings of the European central banks (a key argument of the Rueff school) has similarly been exaggerated. Professor Robert Mossé has shown that between 1958 and 1965 the sum total of these holdings which had been reinvested in New York or London had increased by less than $4 billion, a minute fraction of the total amount of money circulating in

14. Euro-dollars ($10 billion in 1965 and nearly $25 billion at the end of 1958) are dollars held by central banks in both East and West Europe by private industry and individuals, and deposited by them in private European banks. These banks either lend them to other central banks or to American banks or companies. Technically speaking the Euro-dollar system has a two-fold origin. There are higher returns on Euro-dollars than on dollar deposits in banks in the USA, and Euro-dollars can still be borrowed when the sources of credit in the USA are exhausted. Thus the Euro-dollar system has created an international money market which has widened the channels of credit but which has also given impetus to the inflation of international credit and the instability of the international monetary system. It reflects a certain abundance of European capital available for short-term loans to the American capitalist system which can invest it for long-term profits (see Paul Einzig, *The Euro-dollar System*, St. Martin's, New York, 1967, and the Thirty-Eighth Annual Report of the Bank of International Settlements, Basle, 1968). The creation of the Euro-dollar market, centred in London, allows the banks there to continue to play their role as international financiers despite the decline of sterling. In the past, more than half the world's trade was financed in sterling; today it is less than a third. But by acting as intermediaries between lenders and borrowers of Euro-dollars, the bankers of the City of London continue to occupy a place in the centre of the international money market. The Euro-dollar system had also encouraged American banks to set up subsidiaries abroad. There were 105 of these in 1953 and 227 in June 1966.

the USA.[15] It is ridiculous to suggest that such a small sum could be the cause of widespread universal inflation in the world capitalist economy.

The issue of Eurobonds started slowly in 1958 and reached a total of $1·2 billion for the period 1958–62. From 1963 they became considerably more important and the total annual value for the two years of 1963 and 1964 alone was $1·2 billion. The 'interest equalization tax' encourages American subsidiaries to use the Eurobond market. Large-scale borrowing by American corporations started in 1965 and is still growing; $331 million in 1965, 439 million in 1966, 527 million in 1967, and more than 2 billion in 1968, making a total of more than half the $5·35 billion worth of bonds invested in this market between 1963 and 1968 by private companies. (Public institutions have borrowed a further $4 billion over the same period.) At present the Eurobond market absorbs about half the capital entering the European capital market.[16]

To these direct issues should be added the large bankers' credits which American subsidiaries in Europe receive. The estimated value of these credits in 1965 was $1 billion.[17] The same annual level was maintained in 1966, 1967 and 1968. This means that the great American corporations have raised nearly $7·5 billion on the European capital market in the last four years. It would be fruitless to pursue the consequences of this in detail. Skimming off the cream of the European capital market like this has definitely

15. R. Mossé, op. cit., p. 147.

16. The issue of Eurobonds declined in 1969. The total volume went down from $3·3 billion in 1968 to $1·7 for the first eight months of 1969. This reduction was due especially to a drastic fall in issue by private US corporations, starting in the second quarter of 1969. At the same time, bonds issued in German marks overtook those issued in dollars – a clear reflection of the generally anticipated revaluation of the mark.

17. *La Libre Belgique*, 19/20 March 1968.

reinforced the tendency to higher long-term interest rates and to a drop in the rate of industrial profits. During this dangerous period of slowdown in economic growth it has accentuated the shortage of capital and the falling-off of productive investment in Europe, which are in turn related to the recessions in many European nations during this period. Other measures taken by the American central bank network in the last few years to reduce the deficit in the balance of payments have had a similar influence on the situation in Western Europe.[18]

The controversy over the international monetary system between Britain and the USA on the one hand, and France (increasingly supported by the whole EEC) on the other, is not purely academic, but has more and more implications for the evolution of the present economic conjuncture, international as well as European. The shortage of means of international payment together with a world-wide shortage of capital could easily lead to a sudden collapse in the growth rate of international trade and the end of the present boom. Experts who fear this had their beliefs bluntly confirmed by the President of the World Bank at its 1968 session. The vulnerability of the monetary system is also closely linked to the rise of multinational companies. The size of their current capital to hand is often very large compared to that present in many national money markets, and they are able to shift significant sums of capital from one country to another at very short notices.[19]

---

18. *The Economist* (26 November 1966) detailed the relationship between the central banks' tight credit policy and the present recession. The theory of crises explains how an overall shortage in the capital market can go hand-in-hand with increased liquidity on the money market (typified by high interest rates). This liquidity is to some extent the result of the existence of Euro-dollars (see *L'Echo de la Bourse* (Brussels), 28 June 1967).

19. Michael Barratt Brown, *Labour and Sterling*, The Institute of Workers' Control, Pamphlet Series, no. 3, Nottingham, 1968.

The most far-sighted European capitalists recognize that their interests are similar to those of American Capital in this respect, and that these interests demand an extension of the means of international payment, including the development of a world currency ('paper gold'). This would improve the state of international liquidity quite independently of the role of sterling or the dollar. Robert Triffin's proposal to set up 'a central bank of central banks' would have the same effect. It would circulate 'central bank certificates' which would serve as a means of settling international accounts, which could not be used for private dealings or within the national economy.[20]

All such proposals are no more than the expression of the basic fact that the objective socialization of production and international communication is so far advanced that it cries out for a world currency independent of gold. But how can such 'world paper money', which presupposes collective security, exist in an economy based on private property? That is to say, on competition based on each firm's private search for profits, on the compulsion to private capital accumulation, leading inevitably to trade cycles and erratic investments. This is the contradiction the system is unable to solve.

Besides, such a world currency would only postpone the problem of 'secular inflation'; it would not solve it. In the long run it could even make it more explosive.

In any event, a social system which no one can be sure will last into the twenty-first century can obviously not afford the luxury of making long-term plans and considerations the main criteria of its immediate actions. Like the nobility before the French Revolution, whom it resembles in more than one respect, its motto is 'Après nous le déluge!'

20. Robert Triffin, *The World Money Maze*, Yale University Press, New Haven, 1966.

Chapter 9

The Future of
Supranational Institutions

The future of the EEC's supranational institutions ultimately
depends on the extent of the interpenetration of capital in
Europe, with or without Great Britain and other EFTA
countries. Like the formation of the EEC itself, the consolidation of these supranational authorities does not follow
a straight line but is the result of a dialectical process
depending on the struggle between those capitalist groupings which support the interpenetration of capital and those
which oppose it.

We have already shown how national governments rally
to the defence of their own prerogatives and sovereignty,
even where this sometimes entails clashes with the immediate interests of their own capitalists. They will only agree
to surrender important elements of their sovereignty to a
supranational authority if forced to do so by predominant
economic forces in their respective countries.

Closer study of this may indicate under what conditions
and in what circumstances a new European state might be
created. Our starting-point must be the fundamental fact
that the primary role of the bourgeois state is to guarantee
the profits of the great monopolies. We must therefore
begin with a closer examination of that role.

As long as a 'long wave' which is basically expansionist in character prevails, the economic function of the bourgeois state is the classic one of guaranteeing expansion by ensuring a sufficient volume of money and credit and financing public works.[1] Besides this the state in Western Europe can intervene even more directly in the process of economic growth by taking charge of certain investment costs (the nationalized industries, government orders from private companies, subsidies for private investment, etc.), according to the specific structural demands of each national capitalist economy. Overall measures of 'economic programming' – that is, some degree of coordination of investment, production, and sales of the major branches of industry and sections of the economy – can only favour expansion. Special export aid programmes with built-in profit guarantees play a similar role. A combination of these factors alone could be sufficient to extend their influence beyond the national to a supranational European level.[2] In

1. The theory of the 'long wave' formulated by the Russian economist Kondratieff ('Die langen Wellen der Konjunktur', *Archiv für Sozialwissenschaft und Sozialpolitik*, Tübingen, 1926) was extensively used by Josef Schumpeter in *Business Cycles*, McGraw-Hill, New York, 1939. Trotsky also adopted it. In my own article, 'The Economics of Neo-Capitalism' in *The Socialist Register 1964*, ed. Ralph Miliband and John Saville, Monthly Review, New York, 1964, I tried to apply it to the post-war period of capitalist development. Different views of historical causes of economic expansion after the Second World War can be found in Professor Werner Hofmann's *Die säkuläre Inflation*, Duncker und Humblot, Berlin, 1962, Franz Janossy's *Das Ende der Wirtschaftswunder*, Verlag Neue Kritik, Frankfurt, 1968, and in Michael Kidron's *Western Capitalism Since the War*, Weidenfeld and Nicolson, London, 1968.

2. Consider the way European experts have combined national income accounts within the EEC (*Comptes Nationaux, 1955–65*, The EEC Statistical Office, Brussels-Luxembourg, 1966). There are articles on early EEC attempts at more advanced economic planning by Jean Bénard and Vincenzo Vitello in *Tendenze del Capitalisimo Europeo*, Istituto Gramsci, Rome, 1966, and by L. Batti and F. Archibugi, in *Tempi Moderni*, no. 26, Autumn 1966.

an expansionist wave it is not absolutely necessary for big capital to do more than this – it is not yet a question of life and death.

There is no need to analyse here the arguments which support the belief that the long expansionist period is almost at its end. A number of interesting theses have been advanced on this subject, especially by Franz Janossy, relating to the growing delays in training skilled workers, and by Michael Kidron concerning the comparative decline in arms expenditure, or at least the diminishing capacity of armaments to maintain full employment. These factors may be of some importance.[3] They must, however, be subsidiary to the factors decelerating expansion inherent in neo-capitalism itself – the drop in the investment rate as the result of growing excess capacity, the fall in the average rate of profit, and the inability to make up in the long run for the growing gap between productive potential and effective demand by a steadily expanding inflation of credit.

But as soon as this 'long wave' with expansionist tendencies turns into a 'long wave' drifting into stagnation, as soon as annual growth rates decline, and partial recessions – the heralds of generalized recession – multiply in EEC countries, big capital will make heavier demands on the bourgeois state. Counter-cyclical measures, or more exactly, measures to forestall disastrous slumps, will then take precedence over all others. From then on, neo-Keynesianism will again be triumphant. Priority will be given once more to increasing effective demand to boost the

3. Although Kidron exaggerated greatly when he stated in 1967 that 'Western unemployment, except in Britain and France, is near its nadir' at the very moment when unemployment in Western Europe attained its highest point for three years (three million men out of work in the winters of 1966/7 and 1967/8).

economy, or to increasing growth rates by adequate fiscal, financial and monetary policies. Such policies are immediately dependent on two essential factors.

First, it is obvious that as soon as economic integration and the interpenetration of capital within the EEC have gone beyond a certain stage, it will be impossible to operate effective anti-crisis policies within the framework of the *national* economy, which cannot generate the necessary purchasing-power to allow big *European* concerns to maintain profits, and keep up employment while continuing to limit redundancies to a 'reasonable' volume and to sell the major part of their output. Such a policy requires European scale measures, whether the EEC remains as it is or whether it is enlarged.

In late capitalism every bourgeois government is forced to resort to prophylactic or anti-recessionary measures as soon as it is hit by a recession and thereby threatened by a severe economic crisis. The more the economic situation deteriorates, the more important state and governmental intervention in the economy becomes. If national political structures remain unchanged, each separate nation state and each national bourgeoisie will naturally tend to give priority to its own economy. The coordination of international anti-recessionary measures is all the more difficult because these measures are generally inspired by economic nationalism, by the 'sacred egoism' of each national capitalist class. A purely negative ban on these nationalist policies without parallel positive anti-recessionary measures would only increase the likelihood of economic crises.

The steady increase in the scale of the EEC's economic 'programming' tends in this direction. There is a manifest contradiction between ever-increasing economic programming on a national level, with even some indication of real economic planning in the public sector, and ever-increasing interpenetration of capital within the EEC on the other.[4] Ultimately this contradiction can only lead in one of two directions. Either European integration will be reversed, which would amount to a gradual return to economic nationalism (and, in a crisis period, to protectionism), or late capitalism's inherent tendency towards economic programming will pass from a national to a European level, not just quantitatively but in such a way as to bring qualitative, structural changes.[5]

As soon as the EEC finds itself in the grips of a general recession, threatening to spill over into a serious economic crisis, 'European' companies will therefore be forced to demand anti-recessionary policies on a 'European' scale. In other words, they will tend to demand that national governments lose their right to take decisions in critical areas of economic policy and hand over these powers to the supranational authorities of the European Community. The head of Fiat, Gianni Agnelli, told an Italian parliamentary commission in February 1969: 'If we want to introduce systematic programming into the automobile industry, we must act on a supranational level.'

So much for the first of the essential factors. The other is the arsenal of instruments available to make an anti-recessionary or a counter-cyclical policy work. To intervene effectively in the economic sphere, the state requires fiscal, financial, and monetary control. At the same time, increas-

4. This aspect of European economic integration was amongst those discussed by André Gorz, Lelio Basso, Ernest Mandel, Pierre Naville and Jean-Marie Vincent at an international meeting in Paris in early October 1963 (*L'integration européenne et le mouvement ouvrier*, Cahiers du Centre d'Études Socialistes, Paris, 1965).

5. See Ernest Mandel, 'The Economics of Neo-Capitalism' in *The Socialist Register 1964*, Monthly Review, New York, 1964, for a study of the pressures which compel late capitalism to undertake economic programming.

ing European economic integration promotes a growing tendency towards fiscal, financial, and monetary collaboration, which could lead to the creation of a common taxation and budget system, and a common currency. Once this stage has been reached it is no longer possible to deal efficiently with the economic situation at a national level; to be effective, measures have to be carried out at a Community level, supported by supranational authority.

The attempts to create a common European Community currency and a common capital market have left many traces, as countless witnesses – both public and private – can testify. At the end of 1966 the bankers' association of the EEC put forward a memorandum which called for the establishment of a European financial market and outlined how such a market anyway tends to emerge and function spontaneously – for instance, in the above-mentioned loans to North American firms.[6] It should be pointed out in passing that the 'spontaneous' development of this market is closely related to the appearance of an international syndicate created by the great banks. In other words, it corresponds to a specific phase of the interpenetration of capital and simultaneously heralds its next stage.

A group of EEC experts have brought out a report, named after their chairman Claudio Segre, on the conditions for a European capital market, emphasizing how essential it is to establish one. The Segre Report attempts to sweeten the pill for national governments by stressing that a European capital market would not run counter to specific national economic policies – that it is only necessary for the measures which every state takes to regulate credit to be coordinated more closely. The tendency is, however, plain enough. Two years later, the vice-president of the EEC commission,

6. *L'Echo de la Bourse* (Brussels), 13 December 1966.

Raymond Barre, put it even more clearly: 'The Common Market of capital is lagging behind the Common Market of goods because the Treaty of Rome is ambigious on this point and also because of the attitude of the member states who fear that capital mobility will compromise the attainment of their national objectives.'[7]

At the end of November 1966, the European parliament at Strasbourg ratified a motion to set up a common capital market in the EEC, and to coordinate fiscal, financial, and monetary policies in the member states. It also suggested the first steps towards establishing a European currency by striking coins to be valid tender throughout the Six (the one and the five 'Eurofranc' pieces). Robert Marjolin, former member of the EEC Commission, and evidently under pressure from the French government to temper federalist enthusiasm at Strasbourg, argued that completely free movement of capital within the EEC – the first condition of a monetary union – would prevent the member nations from pursuing their own monetary policies. No one could quarrel with that![8]

7. *Le Monde*, 23 November 1968.
8. A similar contradiction can be found in the most recent report of the OECD on improving the European capital market. It foresees a link-up between the various European countries, limited in the first instance to the so-called 'secondary capital market'. This amounts to an open admission that integration which goes any further would threaten the financial sovereignty of national states. But integration limited thus to the 'secondary market' would defeat the object of the European capital market whose purpose is the financing of major European enterprises and companies. The market in Euroloans is in some ways European capital's attempt to impose a capital market, as it were spontaneously, over and above the heads of the member states of the EEC and the Commission. But it is a 'wholesale capital market' and not a 'retail capital market'. Individual capitalists and national firms are virtually excluded; except for large American companies, a few European multi-national corporations on the scale of Philips are its sole beneficiaries.

Two individual opinions on this subject may be cited. The French Minister of Finance under De Gaulle and Pompidou, Valéry Giscard d'Estaing (who is also one of the principal spokesmen of French big capital), speaking in New York before the French Chamber of Commerce, argued for a free, unified European capital market as well as for a common European currency.[9] Louis Camu, president of the board of directors of the second largest bank in Belgium, the Banque de Bruxelles, has emphasized the contradition between the economic integration of the EEC and the national 'egoism' which still dictated monetary and credit policy. He claimed that those who attempted a spontaneous resolution of the contradiction (by issuing shares or raising loans expressed in foreign different currencies simultaneously or in account currency) would in the end force the public authorities to take the initiative of setting up the European capital market themselves.[10]

These witnesses are sufficient. There is obviously a strong tendency in this direction, deriving from the realm of high finance, supported by big business, and defended politically by many different groups. Furthermore, both the need for a more effective counter-cyclical policy and the implications behind a common capital market – let alone a common European currency – call for an increase in the economic and, above all, political integration of capitalist Europe.

In a study published even before the EEC had been formed, Professor Scitovsky pointed out the necessary conditions for the free and effective movement of capital in

9. *L'Echo de la Bourse* (Brussels), 11 December 1966.
10. *L'Echo de la Bourse* (Brussels), 29 June 1966. The same banker has written an interesting article, 'Le marché des Euro-Emissions et les circonstances de son développement', in *La Belgique financière*, a supplement of *AGEFI*, 17 November 1968.

Europe. One of these was a guaranteed and stable rate of exchange, which the monetary alarms of 1968–69 confirmed. (The devaluation of the French franc and two weeks of a floating exchange rate for the German mark wrecked the EEC's common agricultural policy, based on taxes and subsidies which imply fixed rates of exchange between all member countries.)

Besides this, the undesirable social results of international capital concentration could not in the long run be absorbed only by the bourgeoisie of those countries whose capital was diminishing while that of the neighbouring countries increased. Inherent in the common capital market, therefore, is the need to spread the 'social costs' throughout the Community, which cannot be achieved without an effective supranational government. As European neo-capitalism stands at present, a common capital market and a European currency entail an anti-recessionary policy and public works on a European scale, as well as a European employment policy.[11] There is already a demand for a European Investment Corporation which would simultaneously promote such an employment policy (i.e. international socialization of the cost of rationalizing the capitalist economy on a European scale) and European technology.[12] Mr Charles Villiers, managing director of the IRC, speaking at the opening of the Exhibition of West German Industry in West Berlin on 18 September 1969, made an appeal for the creation of Anglo-European industrial combines big enough to compete on a world basis.

11. Tibor Scitovsky, *Economic Theory and Western European Integration*, Stanford University Press, Stanford, California, 1958, pp. 42, 47, 51, 79, 95 *et seq.*

12. Henri Neumann, 'À propos du projet de création d'une Société Européenne d'Investissement' in *La Banque dans le Monde* (a supplement of *L'Echo de la Bourse*), June 1968.

Messrs Grierson (from GEC) and Brooke actually formed a company, Scientific Enterprises Associates, to offer financial aid to medium-sized European firms in order to help them into the world market. Besides the British GEC trust, the Italian Agnelli group, Bosch (the West German group), the Belgian Société Générale, CETIG (the French group), and the English banking houses of Warburg and Rothschild have an interest in this company.[13]

The upshot of this analysis is clear; the EEC's moment of truth will arrive when Europe undergoes a general recession. This will be the decisive test of the Common Market. Either international big capital will be able to bring such pressure to bear on national governments as to force them to make significant concessions at the fiscal, financial and monetary level.[14] In this case there would be a fair chance of applying a counter-cyclical and anti-recessionary policy throughout the Common Market (measures which would be enacted by supranational authority). This would be proof that the EEC had been definitely consolidated and would render the internationalization of private and state capital irrevocable.[15] Such a Community would have as little tendency to revert to the Europe of nation states as the German Reich had to revert to the former individual principalities

13. *The Times*, 18 September 1969, and *L'Echo de la Bourse*, 26 March 1969.
14. Professor André Piettre takes a similar position: 'no European economic union' without 'common European currency' (*Le Monde*, 23 November 1967). Two German authors, Beate Kohler and Gert Schlaeger, have published a book on the same subject: *Ein Markt und eine Währung*, Europa-Union Verlag, Cologne, 1968.
15. The success of an anti-recessionary policy designed to prevent crises can only be temporary. In the long run, capitalism is as intrinsically unable to prevent economic fluctuations as it is to avoid the worsening of recessions. To turn the threat of a severe economic crisis into a milder recession can only be done at the price of inflation. The constant erosion of the purchasing power of the main currencies threatens to shake the world capitalist system to its foundations.

after 1871. The other possibility is that those capitalist circles who persist in defending a national fiscal, monetary and financial policy will triumph, in which case a coordinated anti-recessionary policy throughout the EEC would be impossible. As a severe recession confronts each government, each in turn would put its own anti-recessionary policy into action, which would mean a massive return to protectionism. Consolidation of the EEC will then be out of the question. The entire Common Market will tear itself apart. The weakest European companies will be sacrificed to national 'egoism' and only the strongest will survive, not however as the seeds of a new economic system – a European capitalism – but as foreign bodies within a national economic system, with a role analogous to that played today by American companies. Alongside or together with the latter, they would then doubtless – after long, bitter and painful competition – eventually eliminate 'national' firms.

Such are the conclusions of a general theoretical analysis of the inherent trends of the capitalist economy and of competition between Europe and America – an analysis supported by certain concrete facts. Several member states of the EEC have already experienced recession. The responses of capital and government can be more or less exactly outlined. They roughly correspond to the two alternatives above. In any case, they confirm that, as long as the interpenetration of capital and the transfer of sovereignty to supranational authorities have not gone much further, there is little justification for the assertion that European economic integration is irrevocable.

The French refrigerator industry suffered severely from the establishment of the EEC. Between 1958 and 1966 the total number of manufacturers fell from forty-five to six (of whom three were foreign). Price per cubic capacity halved and this distressing process was accompanied by a partial recession. In 1961 the French manufactured 978,000 refrigerator units, they made 834,000 in 1962, and 953,000 in 1963. Not until 1964 did they exceed the 1961 total with 1·06 million units. While the French industry stagnated or receded, the Italian industry surged ahead. The Italians made 366,000 units in 1957, 977,000 in 1960, 1·53 million in 1963, 2·18 million in 1964 (the year of the Italian recession) and 3 million in 1967. More than 55% of refrigerators sold in France in 1965 were foreign, two-thirds of them Italian. In the first nine months of 1967 80% of refrigerators sold in France had been imported, 75% of them from Italy.[16] The response of French industrial and governmental circles to this invasion has been twofold. As might be expected, there have been industrial mergers; there has also been a return to protectionism.

In 1962 the French introduced 'compensation rights' on refrigerators which had the effect of putting a sizeable tariff on them when they came into France (contrary to the spirit of the Treaty of Rome). The EEC authorities accepted these measures although they limited their duration and extent. On 24 October 1965, just as the period which the EEC had allotted was about to run out, the French government decided to impose quality standards to which refrigerators sold on the French market must conform. As far as Italian and German manufacturers were concerned this was thinly disguised protection for French refrigerator manufacturers. Despite mergers, their products still cost between 15 and 20 per cent more to produce and sell, because – with one exception – foreign manufacturers

16. The four Italian refrigerator manufacturers, Zanussi, Ignis, Indesit and Zoppas had also captured 25% of the British market by the end of the first half of 1967 (*The Economist*, 16 September 1967). They are now establishing a foothold in Canada, from where they intend to invade the US market.

were mass-producing models whose average size was twice that of the French.

The extraordinary success of the Italians in 1967 forced the French government to try to protect its own industry for a third time. On 6 December 1967 it made an official application to the EEC Commission for permission to control the import of electrical household goods into France, and in June 1968, on the pretext of the critical situation in France following the May events, they introduced such measures themselves without waiting for the Commission to make its decision.

This case is not an exception. The Dutch requested special protection for their worsted industry which was threatened by Italian imports. Belgian industrialists sought measures to protect themselves against the import of Italian gas cookers, and they also complained that they were being subjected to unfair competition by Italian sales of stockings, woollens and marble. The Italian motor industry asked for measures to control the import of foreign cars when they believed that the latter were in part responsible for the decline in Italian home sales in 1964.[17]

While the Gaullist regime was vociferously condemned for blind nationalism in opposing the Fiat–Citroën deal, it is just as well to recall that the West German government was also opposed to the merger between Compagnie Française des Pétroles and Gelsenkirchner Bergwerk A.G., which would have formed a powerful 'European' oil trust. The president of the Alsthom group, M. Georges Glasser, recently expressed his disquiet at the appearance, this side

17. The menace of a return to protectionism is not limited to the Common Market area. France, with German encouragement, reduced the amount of Japanese photographic apparatus it imported in 1968 (*Le Monde*, 28/29 April 1968).

of the Atlantic, of large national corporations rather than the formation of European giants. He stated that if this trend persists French industry would obviously be forced to react.[18]

If such protectionist measures are already possible during a partial recession affecting a single branch of industry, or a single country, one can easily imagine what pressures might be brought to bear on governments to impose protective legislation during a general recession. Only in those cases where the international interpenetration of capital has gone so far as to render the interested capitalist factions able to oppose this pressure is it possible to conclude that the Common Market will be able to overcome the decisive test of widespread recession. It is surprising that a Soviet writer, Professor Kirsanov, instead of seeing that the establishment of a European bourgeois state is absolutely dependent on the successful internationalization of capital, stresses instead the absolute primacy of political factors, without even examining what changes would have to be effected in the social infrastructure in order to bring about this new superstructure.[19] 'There have been international monopolies for many years,' he states confidently. 'They come and they go.' But 'international monopolies' which become a *decisive* force in the economy of numerous European nations, and whose break-up would entail the disintegration of the capitalist economy in these countries, obviously constitute a new phenomenon. A 'European capitalist federation' could only appear precisely because of this new phenomenon.

18. *Le Monde*, 17 October 1968. There was considerable alarm in Holland at the beginning of January 1968 because two great European corporations, Mannesmann and Jeumont-Schneider, had showed an interest in buying up stock in the largest Dutch mechanical engineering company.

19. A. W. Kirsanov, *Die USA und Westeuropa*, Akademie Verlag, East Berlin, 1968, pp. 156-7.

Chapter 10

The Working Class
and Inter-Imperialist Competition

Striking changes have taken place in recent years in the attitudes of the two most important classes in bourgeois society towards nationalism and internationalism. Nationalism was initially, in both its progressive and reactionary aspects, a purely bourgeois ideology. Bourgeois society, the achievements of capitalist industry and the rise of the European nations, are all phenomena which, if not exactly synchronous, are closely related to one another. By contrast, the young proletariat was the incarnation of internationalism long before Marx and Engels proclaimed, in *The Communist Manifesto*, 'The working men have no country.'

The reasons why certain mass working-class organizations have become integrated into the bourgeois state cannot be analysed here, but one of the ideological expressions of this integration is undoubtedly their growing disaffection from internationalism. Today, it is worth remembering that not only social democratic, but also communist, and even Maoist organizations think in terms of flying the flag of 'national independence' in the era of late capitalism in the highly industrialized nations of Western Europe, where the fight for this independence reached its climax and fulfilled its historically progressive role one or two centuries ago.

Leaving aside these subjective and ideological factors, there can be no denying that big capital finds it far easier collectively to overcome national barriers than the working class. It is no coincidence that management has been much readier to adapt itself to the far-reaching demands of European economic integration, and has set up many more, and more active, international organs, than has the labour movement.

Naturally, this is to a large extent explained by conjunctural factors and is not a result of the objective situation of the working class. Wage earners in the member countries of the EEC are politically divided, and these divisions have often turned into splits in the trade union movement. Whereas religious or philosophical differences, or the fact that there are conservative, liberal nationalist, cosmopolitan, Jewish and Christian managers, has not prevented the employers setting up a single European institution to represent them, the fragmenting of wage-earners into social democrats, communists, catholics and protestants has so far proved an insuperable obstacle to the formation of a united trade union movement in the EEC.[1]

Over and above these purely conjunctural problems, we must, however, take into account the objective reasons which make it more difficult for wage earners to practise

1. What makes this even more self-contradictory is that branches of the trade union movement like the French Force Ouvrière or the Italian UIL, which are violently opposed to European cooperation with trade unions led by the Italian or French communist parties, are fully ready to recognize the principle of unity of action – and repeatedly practise it with these same unions – at the national level. In other words, these 'convinced Europeans' are prepared to work hand in hand with communist-led unions at home but resolutely refuse to do so on a European scale.

internationalism. The masses cannot acquire internationalism by instinct or by studying it in theory. They can only do so by practical experience and action. The social position of the upper bourgeoisie alone gives it more opportunity to learn foreign languages, to travel abroad, and to keep up contacts with foreign colleagues.[2] The only chance the working class had of meeting its foreign comrades in great numbers was the result of population displacement during and after the tumult of war – not exactly a perfect classroom of international cooperation. Even the potentially positive aspects of the immigration of foreign workers into most of the EEC countries over the last ten years have been neutralized by the objective factors. Insecurity of employment, particularly when there is a threat of economic recession, has made the foreign worker often appear a rival. The worker's lower standard of living, the educational disadvantages he suffers by comparison with the bourgeoisie, have frequently narrowed his horizons, ideas and feelings. He often lacks self-confidence and is therefore instinctively hostile to anything he does not know or finds strange.[3] When powerful proletarian organizations work to raise

2. The situation has changed considerably in recent years because of mass foreign tourism by young workers. The first positive results of this process are already becoming apparent. There is much less prejudice today in Europe against foreign manners and customs, particularly amongst the young. There has also been a vigorous renaissance of internationalism amongst students – a fruit of the student revolt. The revolutionary May events in France witnessed a significant upsurge of international consciousness.

3. This is the psychological background of all forms of racism, not only of anti-semitism, but also of the racist movements directed at Arabs and Africans in France, at Italian immigrant workers in Switzerland, and at coloured people in Great Britain. However, it should be noted that the attempt by Enoch Powell in England to exploit these racist currents politically has so far only found an echo among the most demoralized and backward sectors of the British working class.

levels of consciousness, to attack these tendencies, internationalism certainly can and will be assimilated by the masses as a whole. But, in the last thirty years, it is precisely such an effort that has been lacking in Western Europe. It should be added that the expansion of West European capitalism after the Second World War was made possible by the refusal of these same organizations to exploit favourable conditions in Britain (the Labour landslide of 1945), or the revolutionary upsurge in countries like Italy, France, Belgium, and Greece for the overthrow of the capitalist system.

All this leads to the single conclusion that European big capital was much better prepared to adjust to the organizational consequences of the EEC than was the working class. Employers' federations now exercise a steady influence on the discussions and decisions of the supranational authorities of the EEC, while the West European labour movement has no comparable power to set against it.[4] For this reason the earlier stages of the trend towards European integration had been marked by a decisive shift in the balance of forces, against the wage-earner and in favour of the employer – a shift expressed in the organized labour movement by the parallel gradual surrender by the social democrats of their socialist goals, and the increasing adoption of social democratic positions by the West European communist parties.

An important conclusion regarding political strategy arises from this. There is today no reason why the working

4. In 1958 a list was compiled of employers' federations and trade associations in the six member states of the EEC. Their names filled a book of 513 pages. Jean Meynaud and Dušan Sidjanski in *L'Europe des Affaires*, Éditions Payot, Paris, 1967, pp. 143 and 150, give a description of the various ways in which European companies and employers' federations influence the EEC executive.

class should abandon the classic political goal it has sought for so long – the seizure of power nationally – for the chimerical seizure of power in all member states of the Community at once, or, even more utopian, for the 'socialization' of Europe by the votes of a European parliament elected by universal suffrage.[5] Such a course would only impede the chances of a socialist breakthrough in Europe. The evolution of the social and political forces in the member states of the Community is still governed by the law of uneven development. If the interrelationships between different social forces in a given country are such that conditions are ripe for the workers to seize power, as in May 1968 in France, the law of uneven development operates in favour of socialism once the seizure of power has occurred, and immediately creates a new international situation which changes the relationship of forces in neighbouring countries in favour of the proletariat. If, however, a favourable opportunity is missed on the grounds that neighbouring countries are not yet 'ripe', then the same law starts to operate against socialism, for the betrayal and demoralization then felt by the workers of the country 'ripe' for revolution will reduce it to the same state as those neighbouring countries.

Such considerations, however, should always be based on objective economic factors so as to avoid sterile speculation. The whole analysis of the preceding chapters allows us to conclude that the objective possibilities for a victorious socialist revolution still exist in each member state of the

5. This does not mean that the author has any particular objection to the election of a European parliament by the direct votes of all the inhabitants of the member states as opposed to its present indirect election by the parliaments of the six member states. The point he wishes to make is that in the present economic and political situation no real authority can be exercised by such a European parliament, let alone political power be captured from it – impossible even on a national scale.

Community – given that Capital has not yet formed an effective European union and has not yet set up a powerful European executive endowed with actual state power, especially the kind of power required to put down revolution.

Would a socialist breakthrough disrupt the Common Market? This will ultimately depend on the attitude of the governments of the other countries, on their bourgeoisies and on their working classes, in other words, on the relationship of social forces in all six countries of the Community. Obviously the socialist economy of one member state could not live cheek by jowl with a capitalist economy in the rest of the EEC, but equally obviously the conquest of power by the proletariat of one member state would fan the flames of revolution in neighbouring states. From then everything would depend on the trial of strength on a European scale which a victorious socialist revolution in one Common Market country would unleash. It is evident that it would be much easier to fight from a position *defending* the right of the workers in one country to choose the regime which suits them, without foreign military intervention, economic blockade, or massive withdrawal of capital.

This argument can now be taken to its final conclusions. Once the international interpenetration of capital between the members of the Six leads to their actual economic integration, or to a European Community with more member states, once the supranational institutions evolve an adequately powerful form of state power, then the chances of the proletariat taking power at a national level will probably be insurmountably blocked.[6] The European

6. For this to be so, the foreign ownership of capital, at least as it is usually understood, would not be decisive. After all, successful political and social revolutions have taken place in countries where the majority of capital

working class would then have to adapt its trade union and political activities to a European scale and its institutions would have to be modified accordingly. This is bound to be a complex process, not without regrets and recriminations, which would probably be accompanied initially by a further shift in the relationship of social forces to the disadvantage of the wage-earners. But if objective reality demands this restructuring and re-education of the labour movement, it would be ostrich-like to disregard it. Besides, the element of constraint imposed by such circumstances would itself impel these changes and enable them to be made with the minimum risk.

The reader should not deduce from all this that it is in the interests of the European working class to put a brake on the interpenetration of European capital on the grounds that the gradual disappearance of the possibility of political power being conquered by the working class on a national level, which it ultimately entails, changes the relationship of forces – temporarily at least – to its disadvantage. In the first place, it would anyway be utopian to attempt to prevent economic changes which themselves correspond to a given development of the forces of production; the working class, after all, was never intended to prop up small-scale capitalism or to prevent capital concentration. In the second place, the historical role of the labour movement in late capitalism and in the highly industrialized countries can never consist in allowing itself to be reduced to the status of auxiliary to one or other interest group of the bourgeoisie – either in support of the international interpenetration of capital or to

---

is in foreign hands (Cuba is an example). The crucial factor is the interpenetration of economic, social and political relationships; that is, whether even a provisional return to the nation state is objectively possible and whether the resistance and power of the propertied classes can be neutralized or broken in a country by the revolutionary masses of that country alone.

uphold the bourgeois forces clinging to the nation state. Its role is to place its own socialist aims on the agenda. The alternative to the interpenetration of European capital must be a united socialist Europe, not a return to bourgeois economic nationalism.

The way workers will develop a European consciousness is not by making abstract speeches against nationalism, nor by European congresses, especially if – and this makes them suspect from the start – they are organized jointly with meetings of employers' associations. The true way is by practical and concrete experience, by *actions* carried out on a European scale. As we wrote ten years ago, one strike of European dimensions would do more to give the workers of the EEC a 'European consciousness' than a hundred European congresses. Experience, alas, has subsequently confirmed this in a negative sense.[7]

Increasing international interpenetration of capital is bound to weaken the economic leverage of the trade unions, at least on a purely national level. This weakening will only

---

7. The French miners' strike in 1963 was broken by the import of coal from other EEC and Western European countries without any serious demonstration of solidarity in the neighbouring countries. The long British seamen's strike of 1966 had to get along without any foreign help other than financial support. The strike of women workers at the F.N. factories in Liège in 1966 had even greater significance in the history of the EEC. It lasted about two months and was the first strike aimed expressly at the application of a principle written into the Treaty of Rome – 'equal pay for equal work'. Thus it immediately concerned the interests of women workers in all six member states, but it too had to make do with only 'moral' support, without any political or trade union activity in other firms in the Community. A more recent incident is truly symbolic. During May 1968, while France was in the throes of a general strike, there was an international demonstration in Brussels outside the headquarters of the EEC, for the first time in the history of that institution. But it was not a demonstration of workers but of farmers! These hardened individualists had developed a better practical grasp of collective international solidarity than the labour unions.

be relative as long as this interpenetration is still in its earliest stages. Once it has reached the stage at which quantitative changes entail qualitative changes, that is, once the ownership of the principal means of production is spread throughout all the member states of the EEC, the economic power of national trade unions will to a large extent be broken. A strike of Liège steelworkers would lose most of its effect if ownership of the Liège steelworks were divided throughout the Common Market and if the owners had only had 10% of their capital in the Liège plants. It would then have been in the interest of these capitalists to lose six months' production and profit in Liège, rather than than offer any important concessions to the Liège workers which might rapidly spread to all the steel-producing areas of the EEC.

At present such an idea still seems utopian,[8] though the consequences of the beginnings of international interpenetration of capital and the proliferation of American subsidiaries in Europe have already become very real. Certain sectors of international Capital are able to exploit the different wage levels in different countries and use them to keep wages down overall. We are back at our starting point – the inner logic now governing the export of capital. Naturally, these movements of capital by the great multinational corporations correspond to an economic situation that differs from that which governed the export of capital to backward countries eighty years ago. Political,

8. However, some examples can already be quoted. Ford-Argentine threatened to transfer its activities abroad if the trade unions continued a strike they had called in 1966. Ford/Dagenham threatened to transfer work to Ford/Genck (Belgium) during the March 1969 strike. Ford/Genck itself threatened to transfer work elsewhere and close down the plant when workers in that factory struck against working conditions which were worse than in any other Ford factory in Europe.

fiscal and commercial considerations still play their part, but in the last analysis a world corporation will not allow a subsidiary to continue production longer than it is profitable to do so. Since one can hardly assume that a subsidiary has a higher degree of technology at its disposal than the mother company, the only reason why it can realize a greater-profit is because it pays lower wages.[9] In such circumstances there is nothing to prevent giant corporations, with ramifications everywhere, from switching orders from one country to another if it suits them, blackmailing wage-earners or trade unions whose wages are 'too high', or even closing down some businesses so as to depress wages, and systematically boycotting countries where wages are too high.[10]

Over the last few years the motor industry, too, has shown that the fears caused by this tendency are in no way imaginary. The American automobile workers' union has responded by calling for the establishment of a world-wide automobile union. There is no need to consider here whether such an idea would be feasible or effective, given

9. In the majority of American businesses surveyed, the factors which determined the establishment of plant abroad were lower transport costs, raw material prices, and wage bills (Niels Grosse, 'Amerikanische Direktinvestitionen in Europa', in *Europa Archiv*, 1, 1967.)

10. The *Sunday Times* (26 May 1968) quotes a practical example of the switching of orders from one country to another. The British cotton thread manufacturers, J. & P. Coats, found that their Swedish market was being threatened by the import of cheaper Japanese thread. By shifting their Swedish orders from their British factories to their Japanese ones, they were able to keep their Swedish market. The article in the *Sunday Times* goes on to point out that the first important act of Charles Bell when he became production manager of this firm was to set up a refined system of comparative costing and strict productivity control throughout the world. He said that labour costs vary enormously but that the system was applicable at all wage levels and to any kind of machinery which it might be economica to employ in any given country.

the present structure of the automobile unions in Europe and Japan. The point is that the only successful defence of the working class confronted by growing internationalization of capital is to resort to its own international action and organization.

The first skirmishes and the primary objectives in this new kind of trade union practice should be directed against the multinational trusts (and not only the American ones). European trade unions should now instruct their representatives to develop contacts which can be used for working out common demands, to defend common gains, to organize common actions in order to obtain well-defined objectives, commonly agreed upon and applicable throughout the Community. These steps are an objective necessity for the West European labour movement. The International Metalworkers Federation[11] and the International Chemical Workers Federation which are both affiliated to the ICFTU (International Confederation of Free Trade Unions) made this kind of demand when they asked for international negotiations to get international collective agreements. But this cannot be achieved if the CGT and the CGIL are not allowed to join.[12] Feelers have already been put out for the international negotiations of wages with the world-wide Dutch Philips Corporation. International

11. This covers shipbuilding, the automobile industry, and heavy engineering.

12. CGT: Confédération Générale du Travail (General Confederation of Labour); CGIL: Confederazione Generale Italiana del Lavoro (Italian General Confederation of Labour). There are the two largest trade union federations in their respective countries (France and Italy), and are both affiliated to the left-wing World Federation of Trade Unions (WFTU). As is well known, the ICFTU, which started as a breakaway organization from the WFTU at the height of the cold war, still maintains a rigid anti-communist position and refuses to permit any collaboration between its members and affiliates of the WFTU on an international level.

wage bargaining actually took place in 1968–69 in all the international subsidiaries of the French Saint-Gobain glass trust.[13]

In the gigantic socio-economic metamorphosis which late capitalism is now experiencing – which we may call the third industrial revolution – sections of the working class could suffer as bitter a fate as they did in the first industrial revolution.[14] Fortunately, the working class has learnt from its previous experiences and has a higher level of political organization and consciousness than it had during the first two industrial revolutions; it therefore has a far better chance of defending itself and of winning self-determination and ultimate emancipation than it had at the beginning of the nineteenth and twentieth centuries.

13. *The Economist*, 1 April 1967, and *Le Nouvel Observateur*, 18 August 1969.
14. Paul A. Baran and Paul M. Sweezy in *Monopoly Capital*, Monthly Review, New York, 1966, p. 267, state that according to Willard Wirtz, the American Secretary of Labour, the number of unskilled workers in the USA fell from 13 million in 1950 to less than 4 million in 1962. This is one reason for the higher unemployment rate amongst the black population, especially amongst black youth, and for the increasing militancy of this youth in recent years.

Chapter 11

The Socialist Alternative

Recently an increasing number of technocratic ideologists have tried to persuade the European labour movement that it was in its best interests to integrate itself more thoroughly into the bourgeois state through the supranational institutions of the EEC. This, they claim, is the only effective answer to the increasing influence of American capital in Europe. In France especially, these proposals, advanced by Jean-Jacques Servan-Schreiber, have struck a responsive chord. They are similar to those previously put forward by the Club Jean Moulin (a pressure group of left-liberal and right-wing social-democrat technocrats).[1]

These ideologists direct the same complaints at the partisans of scientific socialism as we have directed at the Gaullists – that in clinging to out-of-date ideas they only hasten the victory of American Capital in Western Europe.

They argue that increasing international concentration and interpenetration of capital is in any case inevitable in Europe, but that it can take two different forms: either the

1. Jean-Jacques Servan-Schreiber, *The American Challenge*, Atheneum, New York, 1969; Claude Bruclain, *Le Socialisme et l'Europe*, Editions du Seuil, Paris, 1965.

absorption of European companies by transatlantic corporations, or the building up of large-scale European corporations. In the first place, the population of Europe loses any possibility of control over the means of production, i.e. the European working class would no longer be able to exert its influence, even indirectly, on management, whether by strike action, demonstrations, or elections. In the second case, it would at least retain these means of indirect influence. For these reasons European wage-earners should consider the international concentration of capital on a European scale, guaranteed by a European federation, as the lesser evil.[2]

Servan-Schreiber's proposals clearly involve an abandonment by the labour movement of its own historical objectives, which he claims are no longer relevant, or anyway, are unobtainable. Only on this assumption can he assert that the labour movement now only has a choice between two forms of capitalist concentration, both harmful to it, and that it will never be in a position to achieve the socialization of major industries.

To give their argument the semblance of truth, Bruclain and Servan-Schreiber use theses presented as self-evident although they do not correspond at all to actual facts. An example is the assertion that economic power is no longer

2. Servan-Schreiber, op. cit., p.153 *et seq.*; Bruclain, op. cit., p. 12 *et seq.* Serge Mallet, the French left socialist, has proposed another variation of this thesis. He has suggested that the working class form a united front with Gaullist 'state capitalist technocracy' against the invasion of Europe by American Capital. This proposal was doubly unrealistic. In the first place because Gaullist strategy was not an effective bar to American Capital, and in the second place because De Gaulle did not represent a 'state capitalist technocracy' but important circles of *private* French big capital. Mallet's proposal would lead the working class to subordinate itself to the interests of one faction of big capital – the goal of ideologues like Servan-Schreiber and Bruclain.

based on property. Connected with this is the other oft-repeated legend that in Sweden – considered the archetypal modern welfare state – inequality of wealth is gradually disappearing because of a progressive reduction in the inequality of earnings.[3] Such theses cannot stand serious scientific analysis. The most important private enterprises in the great capitalist countries continue to be controlled by powerful financial interests whose economic power is based on shareholdings. If such shares only amount to a relatively small proportion of the total capital invested (but always to a very large fortune), as is sometimes the case, this only shows that the capitalist mode of production and centralization of capital now makes it possible for big capitalists to control much more capital than they themselves own. In any case there is no question of economic power being wielded by the 'have-nots', and the so-called managers know this perfectly well. Their ambition is to make the biggest private fortune possible in the shortest possible time by, among other things, exploiting 'inside' knowledge and purchasing stock options.[4]

Anyone who has studied this question knows perfectly well that nearly thirty years of the Welfare State have done almost nothing to reduce economic inequality. 0.1% of the American population still owns over 50% of all shares. In Great Britain 2% of the population owns 55% of the whole country's private wealth, and in Sweden a dozen trusts and financial groups such as Wallenberg dominate the economy in exactly the same way as their American counterparts.

3. Servan-Schreiber, op. cit., p. 245 (and in the Appendix on Sweden in the original French edition, p. 307 *et seq.*); Bruclain, op. cit., p. 151 *et seq.*
4. C. Wright Mills, *The Power Elite*, Oxford University Press, New York, 1957, pp. 117–34 *et seq.*, points out that in the hierarchy of the great American corporations the managers usually never get further than the last but one rung of the ladder.

Even in that petty-bourgeois haven, Denmark, 5% of the households owned over 50% of assessed private wealth in 1966. A thousand 'millionaire' families owned 7·5% of total private wealth in 1953. In 1966 their number had risen to 3,000, but they owned 13% of private wealth, more than that owned by a million of the poorer families put together.[5]

Everyone also knows how expense accounts can be manipulated – in Japan they account for a quarter of gross company profits – and how tax fraud and evasion can be used to wipe out the so-called 'egalitarian' effect of progressive income tax.

There is therefore no objective reason why the West European labour movement should abandon its historical objectives. They are as necessary today as they have been in the past. The economy is still capitalist. Labour power is still

5. The results of numerous studies made in the USA are reproduced in Professor G. William Domhoff's excellent *Who Rules America?* Prentice Hall, New Jersey, 1967. Similar information for Great Britain can be found in Norman Macrae, *The London Capital Market*, Staples Press, London, 1955; Professor Richard M. Titmuss, *Income Distribution and Social Change*, Allen and Unwin, London, 1962, and Professor J. E. Meade, *Efficiency, Equality and the Ownership of Property*, Harvard University Press, Boston, 1964. For the myth of 'Swedish socialism' see, among others, Jean Maynand and Dušan Sidjanski, *L'Europe des Affaires*, Éditions Payot, Paris 1967, p. 179; C. Hermansson, *Monopol och Storfinans* and *Konsentration och Storföretag*, Arbetarkultursförlag, Stockholm, 1962 and 1959; Dr Holger Heide, *Die langfristige Wirtschaftsplanung in Schweden*, J. C. B. Mohr, Tübingen, 1965. During the 1968 election campaign in Sweden, the Social Democrats who had been in power for the previous thirty-six years had to admit that the national economy was dominated by a few groups. Maurice Duverger, in fact, states that control is wielded by 'less than twenty families' (*Le Monde*, 1 November 1968). For the Danish figures, see the *Statistical Yearbook* (published annually in Danish by Det Statistike Department) Copenhagen, 1964.

exploited by private ownership of the means of production. Economic development still follows the inherent laws of the capitalist mode of production. If it did not, the whole process we have described of international competition leading to international concentration of capital would be incomprehensible.

However, it is not even necessary to be a convinced Marxist or a revolutionary socialist to reject Servan-Schreiber's thesis. Technocrats who believe that it is in their political interest to make it more attractive for the labour movement to integrate ever further into bourgeois society not only defy the historical interests of labour but also its immediate material interests.[6]

Servan-Schreiber himself is aware that, according to his theory, the state – in the first place of the supranational European federation – is bound to promote the establishment of great private European companies as much as it can. This is the core of his answer to the 'American Challenge'. He admits that it is reasonable to fear that some of these huge corporations will abuse their economic power. But he answers this objection by saying that the authority of the state must be strengthened against this danger;[7] as if strengthening the monopolies and putting more economic power into fewer hands will not tighten the grasp of these same monopolies on the state! Unless private ownership of

6. Servan-Schreiber describes the need for this integration quite openly. 'The success of other countries suggests that the *fundamental condition* for an industrial society to catch up is a high level of social integration – a kind of peaceful stability . . . that will allow the society to concentrate on the mechanics of change" (op. cit., p. 203).

7. Servan-Schreiber, op. cit., p. 175 *et seq.* Professor Scitovsky has expressed a similar point of view in *Economic Theory and Western European Integration*, Stanford University Press, Stanford, California, 1958, p. 51—that the strengthening of international monopolies as a result of European economic integration will render "open international control" essential.

the means of production is abolished, handing over more power to the state inevitably reinforces the most powerful factions of big capital.[8] Witness the experience of the last thirty-five years, whether under Hitler, Roosevelt or De Gaulle.

Were the working class to follow the advice of these 'left' technocrats, they would not only decisively strengthen their worst class enemies, they would also surrender the most important weapons with which they have defended their own immediate interests in the past – the right freely to negotiate wages, and the open and unrestricted right to strike.

Bruclain and Servan-Schreiber explicitly admit that they are trying to achieve an economic policy of 'stable expansion', which can only work if wages are no longer negotiated by direct bargaining between employers and labour, but are decided by the government or by a 'planning authority', with a ban on unofficial strikes in opposition to their decrees. These steps are designed to guarantee a so-called 'incomes policy'. They try to tone down this fundamentally anti-trade union policy by the assurance that it is not wages alone, but the income of all classes that must come under legal control. This even leads them to make fleeting references to 'an extension of trade union rights'.

8. The following sincere, naïve and cynical statement was published in a financial journal under the suggestive title: 'How to Live with the Giants': 'These men (the directors of big companies) . . . hold the fate of millions of workers in their hands and directly influence the economy of their own country and even of the world. By virtue of their position, they have the ear [sic] of governments. . . . The great directors often get on very well [sic ! !] with the main state officials. This understanding is the product of common background, training, and responsibilities – an ethos combining dynamism and ambition. The result of this mutual understanding is an identity of viewpoints which produces political unity' (*L'Echo de la Bourse* (Brussels), 18 June 1968).

However, in our capitalist society these problems immediately assume a concrete form. Under the conditions dictated by private property, commercial and banking secrecy, and the 'free' market economy, it is impossible for the state or parliament to control prices and profits efficiently. All efforts to achieve such control, some with the assistance of enormous bureaucratic expenditure and outright terror (for example, in the Third Reich) have failed miserably.[9] Whereas it is easy to establish the aggregate amount of wages, there are innumerable ingenious ways by which capitalists can hide profits and increased wealth. The only way in which the actual amount of profit of a capitalist could be precisely determined, let alone limited, would be a radical abolition of commercial and banking secrecy and the institution of workers' control over production, not only at the overall economic and commercial level, but that of every business, factory and workshop too. If it is possible to fiddle the books so as to conceal the true value of stock from a tax inspector, or to disguise the acquisition of new machines as maintenance charges, it is impossible to pull the wool over the workers' eyes in this way, for it is their job to fetch, carry, supervise and use these stocks and work the machinery every day.

The proponents of an incomes policy seem to consider it essential to peg the annual rate of wage increase to the annual increase in productivity so as to maintain the 'stability' of the economy.[10] Significantly enough, demands

9. Between 1933 and 1943, despite many rigorous decrees to hold prices steady, the gross price index of agricultural produce in Nazi Germany rose from 86·4 to 118·6, and that of industrial goods from 117·6 to 149·6 (Charles Bettelheim, *L'économie allemande sous le nazisme*, Rivière, Paris, 1946, p. 211).
10. It should be pointed out in passing that such a limited range of wage increases would tend only to freeze the present division of income between Capital and Labour, which would lead to the stabilization of the rate of

like these are only made during periods of relatively full employment, when employers fear that the law of supply and demand on the labour market will allow certain workers in critical sectors of industry to speed up the rate at which their wages increase. But once there is a recession, if the number of unemployed rises and conditions on the labour market are easier for the employer, the supporters of an incomes policy suddenly forget about their panacea for economic stability. Then they want to leave the fixing of wage rates to negotiations between their 'social partners', if not to 'economic circumstances'. If an incomes policy really were bent upon a 'fair distribution of income', it would raise wages annually *whatever the economic situation*. It would force employers individually or collectively to pay this annual rise to all wage earners, not only in periods of full employment but during a recession as well, whether they are working or unemployed. This would then constitute a guaranteed annual income for all, and the income of the workers would cease to be related to the volume of employment.

One does not need to be a Marxist to see that such an 'incomes policy' is incompatible with the very structure of capitalist society, which regulates wages precisely by cyclical movements of employment. But if the capitalists refuse to disregard the 'laws of the market' when these laws work against Labour, why should Labour agree to the suspension

---

exploitation of wage earners. Not so long ago even moderate trade unionists demanded a redistribution of national income and claimed a greater share of added value for labour. The history of the Welfare State shows that it is utopian to hope for such redistribution by adopting tougher fiscal measures against Capital. The upper bourgeoisie always protects itself against severe income tax and inheritance duties by large-scale tax evasion and fraud. In the copious Anglo-Saxon literature on this subject, Professor Domhoff's *Who Rules America?* cited above, is outstanding.

of these same laws under the exceptional circumstances when they re-establish equilibrium a little at the expense of Capital? 'Economic stability' is not the real goal of the partisans of the 'incomes policy'; what they want is stable and increasing profits. That is why they want 'excessive' wage increases made illegal but not unemployment, or the periodic fall in real wages, or the decline of wage growth rates in periods of recession.

The core of union opposition to these cunningly manipulated campaigns in favour of an incomes policy and 'participation' must be workers' control of production, stretching from the control over actual profits, and the real growth of productivity, to control over the key economic decisions involving investment – and this not only at a national level, but in every branch of industry, in every corporation, and in every factory. This cannot be merely the right to consultation or 'joint control', it must be the right of the elected representatives of the workers to verify and veto anything in all these areas.

Is this the extension of trade union powers to which Servan-Schreiber vaguely refers? Certainly not. The policy we have described would significantly reduce the power and profits of decisive big industries, whereas Servan-Schreiber and others want the exact opposite. As long as the unions and the working class have not conquered these rights, a so-called incomes policy is simply a way of restraining, stopping or even lowering wages. It is nothing less than a redistribution of national income in favour of the property owners at the expense of the wage earners. This conforms exactly with the particularly painful experience of the British working class under the Wilson government.[11]

11. According to *The Economist* (1 July 1967), between June 1966 and January 1967, the first period of severe wage freeze, the nominal weekly income of British workers in seventeen highly important sectors of industry fell between 0·9% for semi-skilled labour in shipbuilding and 7·4% for semi-

Servan-Schreiber's aim, after all, is to raise the profitability of European business to the same level as that of its large American counterparts, and this can only be done at the workers' expense. Such is the purpose behind the fine sentiments of Servan-Schreiber and his cronies. They are asking the European working class voluntarily to abandon the defence of its own interests *vis-à-vis* the great European corporations so that these will be in a better position to defend themselves against transatlantic competition – though there is no need to impose any geographical limits to this discussion. When two large English electrical engineering companies merged, the managing director of one asked trade unionists worried about the danger of redundancies: 'Would you rather we were controlled from Japan?' Thus the ideologists of technocracy try to substitute the idea of the identification of workers with 'their' bosses (national or European) – in other words the idea of competition between the workers which the working class itself rejected over a century ago – for workers' solidarity against Capital.

The same can be said of requests to multinational corporations to invest in one country rather than another. Such requests can only create tensions and divisions between the workers of different countries. This happened recently after the take-over of the Belgian ACEC company, the Italian Marelli company and the French Jeumont company by Westinghouse of America.

Bruclain's and Servan-Schreiber's demand for an incomes policy and their appeal for a strong state and a strong executive have deeper reasons too. These ultimately arise

---

skilled labour in the building trade. The average fall in wages was about 3·5%. If to this is added the rise in the cost of living, officially estimated to be 2·2% but in fact about 3·5%, the Wilson government's incomes policy cost the British working class 7% of their actual income in a mere six months of 'wage restraint'. The British workers tried of course to recoup these losses afterwards.

from the conditions of capital accumulation during a period of accelerated technical development. The rapid depreciation of invested capital requires 'planned investment', in other words, even more intense planning of production costs, which entails planning wage costs too. Besides this it requires increasing socialization of the cost of scientific and technical research. These factors together would lead to further integration; taming of the unions and severe restriction on the right to strike, an increasingly conformist, manipulated and servile bourgeois society, and to the strengthening of an increasingly repressive state, needed to condition the workers to pay the costs of these developments – periodic unemployment, increasing inflation, increasing frustration of artificially aroused needs, increasing intensity of work and exploitation, increasing nervous tension, and increasing ideological and moral debasement – without revolt. The events of May 1968 in France have shown that neo-capitalism has little chance of success. Workers' resistance is mounting and offers a platform for a new strategy which is socialist and anti-capitalist.[12]

12. This is why one cannot agree with the conclusions of Michael Kidron. He claims that mass reformism, indicated by wage-drift, develops its own revolutionary dynamism in opposition to governmental attempts to impose central control of wages (*Western Capitalism since the War*, Weidenfeld and Nicolson, London, 1968, pp. 147–8). These tendencies exist, and, as we pointed out, are the objects of important social conflict. But when a revolutionary situation occurs, the bourgeoisie, apparently unable to make wage concessions under normal circumstances, is willing to concede exceptional wage rises so as to preserve what it considers essential, its control over the factory, the economy and the state. This is what happened in France in May 1968. The only effective working-class response is to aim at the conquest of the state, towards which the creation of organs of dual power is a decisive step. Once again this raises the question of workers' control. Only such a struggle for transitional demands, and not 'mass reformism', can develop revolutionary dynamism under late capitalism.

We should not, therefore, conclude that the European working class ought to be satisfied passively to follow the process of capital interpenetration and international mergers, and only defend workers' jobs and real wages. This narrow syndicalism is no more realistic a way of protecting workers' interests than that offered by the technocracy.

The 'long-wave' of expansion is drawing to its close, to be followed, in Western Europe, by a 'long wave' with a much slower growth rate. The increasing number of branches of industry with excess productive capacity proves that capitalism has been unable to overcome the historical problem of overproduction. In the conditions of 'organized' monopoly capitalism this overproduction can be temporarily 'contained' in over-capacity; but even in this form it cannot help affecting the growth rate of the economy.

In West Germany since 1960 manufacturing industry has shown a marked tendency to underemploy its productive capacity so that by the end of 1967 the rate of utilization had fallen below 80%. Since 1958 a similar trend has been prevalent in the food and luxury goods industries.[13] In France on the eve of the May explosion industry was only working at 75% capacity.[14] In mid 1969 US industry was operating at 83% of its capacity, compared with 91% in 1966, at the peak of the boom. After coal-mining, the steel industry has now reached a state of chronic structural over-capacity in Western Europe and North America. For several years, less than 80% of the productive capacity of these plants in the Common Market has been in use. The same

13. *Jahresgutachten 1967 des Sachverständigenrates zur Begutachtung der gesamtwirtschaftlichen Entwicklung*, p. 59. The significance of this is that the severe credit deflation which the German Federal Bank introduced was not the real cause of the 1966/67 recession; it only hastened its onset in order to limit its extent.

14. *The Times*, 28 May 1968.

phenomenon is spreading to the motor and petrochemical industries,[15] and is even more marked in the plastics industry. In other words, security of job tenure under capitalist production is more and more proving itself to be a chimera.

On the other hand, the new industrial revolution has not only profoundly modified the structure of employment, but also that of consumption and specifically the relations between individual and social consumption, in the same way that it has modified the conditions for the reproduction of labour power.

Socialists have never ceased to point out that capitalism is not only unjust, it is also irrational. This irrationality is expressed most clearly in the colossal waste of human labour and mechanical means of production caused by underemployment, wars, arms manufacture and the unequal distribution of income and property. This is how it was and still is. The amount of waste has not diminished one whit.[16]

As well as this classical capitalist waste, there is now a new kind of waste which, in the coming years and decades, will take ever more catastrophic forms. Capitalism not only

15. *The Economist*, 30 September 1967. This is why the American chemical trust, Du Pont, started a price war in Great Britain by substantially cutting the cost of Orlon and Dacron. First cuts were in June 1967 and a second of 18% took place in August of the same year (*The Economist*, 2 September 1967). An article on this topic was also published in the *Financial Times* (29 July 1968) entitled 'Plastics haunted by overcapacity'. The new petrochemical complex at Antwerp should be ready by 1970 to produce more than 3 million tons of finished goods; that is more than the entire European plastics production in 1960.

16. It is true that post-war recessions have depressed production 'only' by between 5 and 15% instead of between 20 and 35% as the 1930 crisis did. But, in the first place, this lower percentage refers to a much larger aggregate than in the past, and secondly, there is the additional waste of economic resources inherent in the enormous arms expenditure (at present $70 billion a year in the USA alone), which bears no relation to that of the thirties.

wastes society's resources by *not* employing men and machinery; by employing them *senselessly* it increases this waste even more.

The more the productive capacity of partially or fully automated large-scale industry increases to a dizzy height, the harder it becomes to realize the surplus value inherent in the commodities it produces and the higher their distribution and sales costs become, which are already surpassing actual production costs.[17] Simultaneously, the production of useless goods or goods of intentionally inferior quality increases – anything to enable the productive apparatus to keep going.[18]

When bourgeois authors, prejudiced in favour of the market economy, speak of the 'truly affluent society' of the future, they literally mean a society in which every house-

17. The Brussels stock exchange paper, *L'Echo de la Bourse* (20 December 1967), reported that the cost of producing and delivering an average Italian refrigerator to the Italian frontier (in other words, including a part of the transport and delivery charges) had fallen to below 250 French francs. The production cost could be estimated to be 200 French francs, i.e. 43 US dollars. This figure should be compared with the average retail price of such refrigerators.

18. Vance Packard, *The Waste Makers*, David McKay Co., New York, 1960; Adolf Kozlik, *Der Vergeudungskapitalismus*, Europa Verlag, Vienna, 1966. Bowden has condemned the wastefulness of the space race in the USA in *Les Temps Modernes*, May–June 1968. The irrationality of the system not only explodes at this macro-economic level but threatens the very survival of mankind at a 'macro-social' level, with the disintegration of the great cities, the pollution of air and water, and with the rise of mental illness and alcoholism in the richest capitalist countries. Even the disposal of 'waste' in the literal sense of the word has become a growing difficulty. In September 1969, the *Nation* reported that American citizens are at present throwing away 720 billion pounds of garbage per year, not including 6 trillion pounds of mineral and agricultural solid wastes. The 'disposal costs' of this garbage are estimated at $4½ billion annually, a sum exceeded in the civilian budget of the USA only by expenditure on schools and roads.

hold possesses ten refrigerators.[19] This gigantic stockpile of things goes hand in hand with the increasing neglect, frustration and mutilation of human beings. The producers suffer first and foremost – imprisoned in hierarchical and oppressive factories, their talents, dignity and personality stunted and all their creative faculties withered. This contradiction becomes increasingly absurd and increasingly explosive as the development of technology dictates an ever higher level of education for these very producers.

The trajectory of the modern forces of production drives beyond the boundaries of the nation state and private property; these forces must eventually break free from the shackles of capitalist production and appropriation. Contemporary technology, cybernetics and nuclear energy demand the free, planned and conscious association of producers and consumers on an international scale. Genuine economic democracy presupposes an economic system in which the choice of what to produce, the decisions on how much and where to invest, and the extent of the consumer sacrifices to be borne by every sector of society are established after democratic discussion by the masses who are themselves concerned, and not behind their backs either by the blind, impersonal *diktat* of the market, by a dictatorial gang of business and financial magnates, or by an allegedly omniscient politbureau.[20]

This contradiction can be grasped in two ways. In the

19. François Hetman, *L'Europe de l'abondance*, Editions Fayard, Paris, 1967.

20. Contrast this with the situation in Great Britain where a small body of British and international financiers imposed substantial cuts in social spending after the devaluation of sterling, against the express wishes of the majority of the electorate. This is an excellent example of what passes for democracy in the West. *The Economist* (24 February 1968) reported that the IMF had imposed what amounted to a veto on the amount of public spending in relation to the national budget.

first place, there is an *economic* contradiction; the relative abundance and saturation in many consumer areas of industrialized capitalist countries make rigid adherence to the market economy absurd.[21] It also clashes violently with the growing needs of the so-called Third World. In the second place there is a *social* contradiction: increasing automation further accentuates the authoritarian structure of factories, firms and society as a whole, and at the same time provokes a growing reaction against it, which is spurred on by higher levels of education and work skills.[22] When industry has been entirely automated, which 'futurologists' estimate will occur by the end of this century, these contradictions will be strained to the limit. Workers and intellectuals will be faced with the following choice: either passively to accept an authority which will have been strengthened beyond our imagination by a monopoly of access to the enormous mass of information centralized in the computers – in other words to accept a steady erosion of the last

21. Even a bourgeois liberal like Galbraith admits this; see *The Affluent Society* and *The New Industrial State*. Servan-Schreiber (op. cit., pp. 196–8) repeats the views of that component of the American Establishment, Herman Kahn, who states that the market economy is in permanent recession due to technological progress. But he fails to draw any political or social conclusions for Western Europe from this obvious fact.

22. In 1964 half the 2,500 strikes which took place in Great Britain and 40 per cent of the 2·3 million lost working days were caused by disputes about the internal structure of industry (*The Incompatibles*, Robin Blackburn and Alexander Cockburn, eds., New Left Review and Penguin Books, Harmondsworth, 1967). The Institute for Workers' Control, which is extending its influence on the British Left, recently published a collection of articles under the title *Can the Workers run Industry?* (Sphere Books, London, 1968). The drive towards workers' control was also evident during 1968, in the Fiat and Pirelli factories in Italy, and in several occupied factories in France during the strikes of May / June. In September 1969, three GEC plants in Liverpool came within an inch of the first strike for workers' control involving factory occupation in the history of the Western European labour movement.

democratic liberties and surrender to the absurd union between despotic, technocratic capitalism and the anarchic market economy; or else to solve these contradiction on the basis of socialist planning, designed to satisfy human needs and not those of capital accumulation and the realization of profits – in other words to introduce a system of planning based on democratically centralized workers' self-management.[23]

What we called the third industrial revolution, bringing with it increased international competition and interpenetration of capital, is bound to result in an intensification of conflict between workers and employers. In the growing proletarian opposition to incomes policies, wage restraint, anti-trade union legislation and limitations on the right to strike; in their resistance to recurrent unemployment, 're-dundancies', mass lay-offs and periodic closures of factories; and in their revolt against their alienation as producers and consumers as well as the fundamental inequalities of wealth and economic power, workers will acquire the consciousness, the militancy, and the organization necessary to turn general strikes such as those in Belgium in 1960–1 and in France in 1968 into struggles leading to the conquest of power and the breakthrough to socialism.

This socialist alternative is the key to the solution of the problems raised by the competition between Europe and America. Both forms of international capital concentration, the interpenetration of capital within Europe and the mergers between European and American Capital with the latter in charge, profoundly contradict the demands of modern

23. The reason such a system is *economically* more rational than a market economy is that costs (both economic and social) could dictate the prior allocation of human and material resources, and that these priorities, too, would be determined democratically by all those concerned.

technology, and the establishment of a more humane society. Bourgeois economists have made the chilling prediction that within a few years the whole economy of the West will be dominated by three hundred multinational trusts.[24]

The socialist answer to that prediction is that we do not wish to choose between three hundred American or three hundred European masters to govern 350 million Europeans. We would rather see European labour, free from all masters, organized in a free association of producers. Only such cooperation is capable of exploiting the potentialities of modern technology to the full and for the benefit of all mankind.

All such perspectives are ignored by such authors as John Pinder, Roy Pryce, and the contributors to *Science and Technology in Europe*,[25] who have discovered, with belated enthusiasm, the competitive potential of large-scale European companies and the economic momentum of technological progress, without giving much thought to the heavy social price exacted by them under capitalism. They seem oblivi-

24. Philip J. Barber, 'Les entreprises internationales' in *Analyse et prévision*, September 1966. Professor Perlmutter of the Centre for Industrial Research in Geneva has made a similar estimate (*The Economist*, 13 July 1968). In Spring 1968 a Special Committee of the Transnational Society was inaugurated in Paris under the initiative of Arthur Watson of the American IBM corporation. The Chairman, Wilfried Baumgartner, was a former Governor of the Banque de France and is currently President of the main French chemical trust, Rhône-Poulenc. *L'Echo de la Bourse* (Brussels), 28 May 1968, reported that at the opening session it was predicted that in a few years time two-thirds of the industrial plant of the 'Free World' would be in the hands of multinational companies. These businessmen seemed to be unaware of the fact that a world dominated by three hundred tycoons could hardly be called free.

25. John Pinder and Roy Pryce, *Europe After De Gaulle*, Penguin Special, Baltimore, 1970, pp. 101–13ff.; Eric Moonman (ed.), *Science and Technology in Europe*, Penguin Special, Harmondsworth, 1969.

ous of the fact that the transformation of Europe into a second America does not offer such a bright prospect after all, entailing – alongside the technological achievements – public squalor, mass poverty, and tremendous waste. Pinder's naïve confidence that state initiatives, as in Sweden or Italy, could overcome the 'pain and inconvenience' of large-scale uneven development in integrated capitalist Europe is not borne out by experience; despite twenty years of such 'state initiative' in Italy, the inequality of income between the North and the South has increased and not diminished.

Does the 'American Challenge' suggest that Europe has lost its chance for socialism? Servan-Schreiber and Bruclain fail in any way to prove their claim that socialization of the great European firms would provoke such an acceleration of the flight of scientists and technologists to the United States that the technological gap between Europe and America would then widen. The claim rests on the misanthropic idea that the only factor which determines where and how a man will work is money. That this is far too pessimistic is partly proved by the fact that British nuclear physicists have achieved tremendous success on much less pay than their American counterparts, and so have the space scientists of the Soviet Union.[26] Even if their pessimism

26. The establishment of powerful 'European' industrial companies is no guarantee that technological innovation will be intensified in Europe. *The Economist* (7 December 1968) reports on carbon fibres, a British discovery. This is a material four times stronger and at the same time four times lighter than steel. It was developed by the RAF at Farnborough, by the UKAEA and Rolls-Royce, and promptly sold under licence to an American company by Rolls-Royce so as to be manufactured in the USA and to capitalize on the American market to the full. As long as there is capitalism, the desire for profit will take precedence over every other factor, and certainly over 'European nationalism'.

were true of this generation of scientists, socialist Europe would have two substantial advantages to help it catch up with American technology.

At the moment, in Britain, West Germany, France and Italy between 90 and 98% of the children of workers cannot go to university. A thorough social revolution with economic planning and the minimization of wasted human and material resources would enable between 30 and 40% of these children to get higher education. There would be a phenomenal upsurge of scientific and technical creativity and this – under democratic socialism – would be far and away superior to any conceivable development of 'organized' capitalism. Secondly, scientific and technical research in the USA is fundamentally limited by its utilitarianism and by its ties with military objectives. Even today Europe leads in pure, basic research.[27] In the long run it is this pure research which produces the technical breakthroughs. If society was based on planned workers' control and enjoyed a huge extension of genuine democracy, it would be able to create a framework of basic research which would carry it far beyond the profit-orientated research of the USA.[28] Chalfont's frivolous proposal to blackmail the

27. See the article cited above by Klaus-Heinrich Standke in *Europa Archiv*, No. 16, 1967, on the technological gap between Europe and America.

28. It is significant that big capital's most intelligent supporters have realized that utilitarian research, especially profit-related research, has a deleterious effect on scientific progress and development as a whole, whereas so-called 'socialists' – in fact supporters of technocracy – seek their salvation in the spreading of the profit motive. This is the real significance of David S. Smith's remarks, made when he was vice-president of Philco corporation: 'Most companies find it desirable to have a separate research group – completely divorced from current problems and normally charged with the objective of undertaking speculative research in the hope that it will lead to technical breakthroughs that form the basis for growth by innovation. It is not logical to consider such a group a profit centre, since they are rather

Common Market by proposing that the USSR and other Eastern countries join a 'technological community' might then even be looked upon as a serious provisional solution until the next generation of socialist intellectuals had fully developed. Furthermore, a socialist Europe would be able to offer the 'Third World' the kind of cooperation and disinterested friendship which no imperialist country of the capitalist world can provide;[29] it would thereby gain a solid alliance with more than two-thirds of mankind.

When the socialist labour movement determines its tactics towards the rivalry between European and American Capital it should remember that *capitalism* is ultimately the American 'Trojan Horse' in Europe.[30] In the last resort we are left with a choice between direct subjection to American capitalism and indirect 'Americanization', i.e. subjection to methods of mass manipulation and increasing alienation of workers, introduced with the pretext of offering more effective competition against American capital.

Between the devil of subjection to America, and the deep blue sea of 'Americanization', socialism offers us the only clear way out. Forward, against American and European monopolists, to the United Socialist States of Europe!

---

remote from the actual pay-off. Indeed it is necessary to insulate such a group from concern with current problems or immediate return on their effort if they are successfully to accomplish their objective of innovation' (*Technological Planning on the Corporate Level*, ed. James R. Bright, Harvard University Graduate School of Business Administration, Boston, 1962, pp. 35–6).

29. This is without considering how attractive such a radical but free socialist Europe would be to American workers and intellectuals.

30. The expression was originally coined by the French political scientist, Maurice Duverger (*Le Monde*, 29/30 October 1967).

Bibliography

Books and Articles

Archibugi, F., 'La Definizione degli obiettivi della programmazione europea' in *Tempi Moderni*, no. 26, Autumn 1966.

Bain, Joe S., *International Differences in Industrial Structure*, Yale University Press, New Haven and London, 1966.

Baran, Paul A. and Sweezy, Paul M., *Monopoly Capital*, Monthly Review Press, New York and London, 1966.

Barber, Philip J., 'Les entreprises internationales' in *Analyses et Prévisions*, September 1966.

Barratt Brown, Michael, *After Imperialism*, Hillary House, New York, 1963.

Barratt Brown, Michael, *Labour and Sterling*, The Institute of Workers' Control, Nottingham, 1968.

Basso, Lelio; Gorz, André; Mandel, Ernest; Naville, Pierre; Vincent, Jean-Marie, 'L'integration européene et le mouvement ouvrier' in *Cahiers du Centre d'Études Socialistes*, Paris, 1965.

Batti, L., 'Il programma di politica economica a medio termine' in *Tempi Moderni*, no. 26, Autumn 1966.

Bénard, Jean and Vitello, Vincenzo, in *Tendenze del Capitalismo Europeo*, Istituto Gramsci, Rome, 1966.

Bettelheim, Charles, *L'économie allemande sous le nazisme*, Rivière, Paris, 1946.

Blackburn, Robin and Cockburn, Alexander, eds, *The Incompatibles*, Penguin Books and New Left Review, Harmondsworth, 1967.

Bloch-Laîné, F. and Perroux, François, *L'entreprise et l'économie au XXe siècle*, vol. 1, Presse Universitaire de France, Paris, 1966.

Bowden, Lord, 'Inflation scientifique et fuite des cervaux' in *Les Temps Modernes*, May–June 1968.

Bright, James R., ed., *Technological Planning on the Corporate Level*, Harvard University Graduate School of Business Administration, Boston, 1962.

Brown, A. J., *Introduction to the World Economy*, Allen and Unwin, London, 1966.

Bruclain, Claude, *Le Socialisme et l'Europe*, Éditions du Seuil, Paris, 1965.

Coates, Ken, ed., *Can the Workers Run Industry?*, Sphere Books, London, 1968.

Cook, Fred J., 'Juggernaut, the Warfare State' in *The Nation*, 20 October 1961.

Domhoff, G. William, *Who Rules America?*, Prentice Hall, New Jersey, 1967.

Dunning, J. H., *American Investment in British Manufacturing Industry*, Allen and Unwin, London, 1958.

Freeman, C. and Young, A., 'The Research and Development Effort in Western Europe, North America and the Soviet Union', OECD, Paris, 1965.

Galbraith, J. K., *The Affluent Society*, 2nd ed., Houghton Mifflin, Boston, 1969.

Galbraith, J. K., *The New Industrial State*, Houghton Mifflin, Boston, 1967.

Granick, David, *The European Executive*, Weidenfeld and Nicolson, London, 1962.

Grosse, Niels, 'Amerikanische Direktinvestionen' in *Europa Archiv*, 1, 1967.

Heide, Holge, *Die langfristige Wirtschaftsplanung in Schweden*, J. C. B. Mohr, Tübingen, 1965.

Hermansson, C. H., *Konsentration och Storföretag*, Arbetakulturs Förlag, Stockholm, 1959.

Hermansson, C. H., *Monopol och Storfinans*, Arbetakulturs Förlag, Stockholm, 1962.

Hetman, François, *L'Europe de l'abondance*, Éditions Fayard, Paris, 1967.

Hofmann, Werner, *Die säkuläre Inflation*, Duncker und Humblot, Berlin, 1962.

Hymer, Stephen, 'Direct Foreign Investment and International Oligopoly' (unpublished typescript), 1965.

Janossy, Franz, *Das Ende der Wirtschaftswunder*, Verlag Neue Kritik, Frankfurt/M., 1969.

Kahn, Herman, *Report on the Year 2000*, Macmillan, New York, 1967.

Kidron, Michael, *Western Capitalism since the War*, Weidenfeld and Nicolson, London, 1968.

Kirsanow, A. W., *Die USA und Westeuropa*, Akademie Verlag, East Berlin, 1969.

Kitzinger, Uwe W., *The Politics and Economics of European Integration*, Praeger, New York, 1964.

Kohler, B. and Schlaeger, G., *Ein Markt und eine Währung*, Europa-Union Verlag, Cologne, 1968.

Kondratieff, N., 'Die langen Wellen der Konjunktur' in *Archiv für Sozialwissenschaft und Sozialpolitik*, Tübingen, 1926.

Kozlik, Adolf, *Der Vergeudungskapitalismus*, Europa Verlag, Vienna, 1969.

Layton, Christopher, *European Advanced Technology*, PEP, London, 1969.

Lopez, Muñoz, Arturo, and Delgado, José Garcia, *Crecimiento y Crisis del Capitalismo español*, Cuadernos para el Dialogo, Madrid, 1968.

Macrae, Norman, *The London Capital Market*, Staples Press, London, 1955.

Magdoff, Harry, 'Problems of United States Capitalism' in *The Socialist Register*, Monthly Review Press, New York, 1965.

Magdoff, Harry, *The Age of Imperialism*, Monthly Review Press, New York, 1969.

Magistrelli, F. and Ragozzini, G., 'Gli Investimenti americani in Europa' in *Problemi del Socialismo*, November/December 1965 and July/August 1966.

Mallet, Serge, *La nouvelle classe ouvrière*, Éditions du Seuil, Paris, 1963.

Mandel, Ernest, *Marxist Economic Theory*, Monthly Review Press, New York, 1969.

Mandel, Ernest, 'The Economics of Neo-Capitalism' in *The Socialist Register*, Monthly Review Press, New York, 1964.

Mandel, Ernest, 'La réforme de la planification soviétique et ses implications' in *Les Temps Modernes*, June 1965.

Marx, Karl, *Wages, Price and Profit*, Foreign Language Publishing House, Moscow, n.d.

Marx, Karl, *Capital*, Lawrence and Wishart, London, 1965.

Marx, Karl and Engels, Friedrich, *Werke*, vol. 36, Adler, New York.

Marx, Karl and Engels, Friedrich, *Selected Correspondence, 1846-1895*, International Publishers, New York, 1942.

Meade, J. E., *Efficiency, Equality and Ownership of Property*, Allen and Unwin, London, 1964.

Melman, S., *Our Depleted Society*, Holt, Rinehart and Winston, New York, 1965.

Meynaud, Jean and Sidjanski, Dušan, *L'Europe des affaires*, Éditions Payot, Paris, 1967.

Mills, C. Wright, *The Power Elite*, Oxford University Press, New York, 1956.

Moonman, Eric, *Science and Technology in Europe*, Penguin Books, Harmondsworth, 1969.

Moore, Geoffrey, 'Measuring Recession' in *The Journal of the American Statistics Society*, June 1958.

Mossé, Robert, *Les problèmes monétaires internationaux*, Éditions Payot, Paris, 1967.

Naville, Pierre, *La classe ouvrière et le régime gaulliste*, Études et Documentations Internationales, Paris, 1964.

Nogaro, Bertrand, *La monnaie et les systèmes monétaires*, Librairie de Droit et de Jurisprudence, Paris, 1948.

Packard, Vance, *The Waste Makers*, David McKay, New York, 1960.

Pen, J., *Harmonie en conflict*, Kritische Biblioteek, Amsterdam, 1968.

Pinder, John and Price, Roy, *Europe After De Gaulle*, Penguin Books, Baltimore, 1970.

Prager, Theodor, *Wirtschaftswunder oder keines?* Europa Verlag, Vienna, 1963.

Rappard, William E., *The Secret of American Prosperity*, Greenberg, New York, 1955.

Robinson, Joan, *Economic Philosophy*, Doubleday/Anchor, New York.

Rothschild, Kurt W., *Marktform, Löhne, Aussenhandel*, Europa Verlag, Vienna, 1966.

Rueff, Jacques, *L'age de l'inflation*, Éditions Payot, Paris, 1963.

Safarian, A. E., *Foreign Ownership of Canadian Industry*, McGraw-Hill, Toronto, 1966.

Schumpeter, Josef, *Business Cycles*, McGraw-Hill, New York, 1939.

Schumpeter, Josef, *Imperialism and Social Classes*, Augustus Kelly, New York, 1951.

Scitovsky, Tibor, *Economic Theory and Western European Integration*, Stanford University Press, Stanford, California, 1958.

Servan-Schreiber, Jean-Jacques, *The American Challenge*, Atheneum, New York, 1967.

Simon, Herbert A., *The Shape of Automation for Men and Management*, Harper & Row, New York, 1966.

Southard, F. E., *American Industry in Europe*, Houghton Mifflin, Boston, 1931.

Standke, K-H., 'Die Technologie-kluft' in *Europa Archiv*, 16, 1967.

Sweezy, Paul M. and Huberman, Leo, 'Gold, Dollars and Empire' in *Monthly Review*, February 1968.

Titmuss, Richard, *Income Distribution and Social Change*, Allen and Unwin, London, 1962.

Triffin, Robert, *The World Money Maze*, Yale University Press, New Haven, 1966.

Trotsky, Leon, *Europe and America*, Fourth International Publications, Colombo, 1943.

Truman, Harry S., *Year of Decision*, Doubleday, New York, 1955.

Uri, Pierre, ed., *From Commonwealth to Common Market*, Penguin Books, Harmondsworth, 1968.

Uri, Pierre, and others, ed., *Les investissements étrangers en Europe*, Éditions Dunod, Paris, 1967.

Vilmar, Fritz, *Rüstung und Abrüstung im Spätkapitalismus*, Europäische Verlagsanstalt, Frankfurt/M., 1965.

Wall, Edward, *Europe: Unification and Law*, Penguin Books, Harmondsworth, 1969.

Wells, Sidney, *Trade Policies for Britain*, Chatham House Essays, London, 1966.

Miscellaneous Documents

Bank of International Settlements, *Thirty-Eighth Annual Report*, Basle, 1968.

Hearings by the Senate Subcommittee on Antitrust and Monopoly of the Committee of the Judiciary, *Concentration in American Industry*, U.S. Government Printing Office, Washington, 1957 and 1964.

Hearings before the Joint Economic Committee Congress of the USA, *Economic Report of the President : January 1962*, U.S. Government Printing Office, Washington, 1962.

Institut d'Administration des Entreprises de l'Université de Paris, *Les ententes a l'échelle européene*, Éditions Dunod, Paris, 1967.

Les investissements étrangers en Europe, Éditions Dunod, Paris, 1968.

OECD, *The Overall Level and Structure of Research and Development Efforts in OECD Countries, 1963–64*, OECD, Paris, 1965.

Statistisches Amt der Europäischen Gemeinschaften, *Volkswirtschaftliche Gesamtrechnung*, Brussels/Luxemburg, 1966.

UN World Economic Survey, New York, 1963.